Chief Justice

# Ranjan Gogoi

C

.Sabarimuthu. V                    Volume 1

Chief Justice

# Ranjan Gogoi

VOLUME 1

This book deals with the first 121 days in office

of

Justice Mr. Ranjan Gogoi as the Chief Justice of India.

## <u>Dedication</u>

**My maternal uncle, Mr. R. Maria Michael, who stood like  a rock to educate me after my first year college.**

## All Rights Reserved

I authorize the Amazon.com to print and market this book. It shall not be reproduced in any form by any others without the prior permission of the author.

V. Sabarimuthu

Author

9-2-2019

Revised on 15-8-2019

# Volume Table of Contents
## Volume 1

Contents

# PREFACE

On January 12, 2018, *Justice Ranjan Gogoi* and three other judges came out of the Supreme Court of India, convened a press meet and alleged that democracy was not safe in the hand of the then Chief Justice of India, *Dipak Misra*, They disclosed that 'many things that were less than desirable were happening in the Supreme Court of India and unless that institution is saved, democracy would not survive in India". Further, they said the Chief Justice of India was not functioning independently but was remote controlled.

Everyone thought that *Justice Ranjan Gogoi* would use his talents to serve the country with his judgement the moment he becomes the Chief Justice of India. Many said that he would give life to the nation.

In the Union of India Vs democratic reforms, in 2002, a bench of the Supreme Court of India said that 'one sided information, disinformation, mis-information and non-information all equally create an uninformed citizenry which make democracy in India a farce'.

The source of the authority of the Chief Justice of India is the Constitution of India.

Hence, the Chief Justice of India is the most powerful person in India. He must ensure rule of law, freedom of expression and democracy. He must uphold the constitutional rights of the people. Thus, he must enforce the constitution of India. His accountability, therefore, must be the greatest. Similarly, the greater the responsibility, the greater the risk associated with it.

When the system violates Article 19, the Chief Justice of India must stand erect and point out that the restrictive clauses would not undo freedom of expression.

Yet, the Supreme Court of India did not enforce freedom of expression for the last 17 years. Thus, it did violence against Articles 19 without the slightest compunction.

If the Central Bureau of Investigation (CBI) promotes corruption, the court would not interfere. If it prevents corruption, it would interfere. It conveys the impression, that the Supreme Court of India exists only to pervert justice. This condition prompted Union Finance Minister Mr. Arun Jaitely to say that 'the violation of the Constitution of India is a question of the credibility of the court'.

As soon as assuming office, Chief Justice of India Ranjan Gogoi said, "It is in our best interest to heed the advice of the Constitution of India. If we do not, our hubris will result in sharp descent into chaos" When he said this, the court had frozen 647 letters from the present man alone" His words gave the impression that he was facing resistance from the media.

During the Rafale hearing, the bench headed by him directed the Government to inform **the decision-making process** that led to the *Rafale agreement.*

During the farewell function of Justice Kurian Joseph, Chief Justice of India Ranjan Gogoi said that the judges were fast losing the honor and majesty of office.

On 26 November 2018, quoting John Sturt Mill, he said **"Don't leave your liberties at the feet of even a great man"**.

His deeds and words prompted the Attorney General of India, K,K, Venugopal, that the Chief Justice of India was not above the law.

The present man sent 55 letters to the Supreme Court of India for the freedom of Indians since *Chief Justice of India Ranjan Gogoi* assumed office on 3 rd October 2018. But he omits to state this material fact to the illiterate people of India.

These letters are necessary to the voters to take a balanced decision at the time of voting.

However, they do not know such omission on the part of the Chief Justice of India.

He knew that his such untruth or omission to state the material facts would mislead the people to vote in favor of two persons accused of violating Article 19 of the Constitution of India. He knew that such omission on his part would make him liable to all Indians.

# 1

# A dark secret

The President of India is taking away the 'life' and 'liberty' of the people by concealing the letters of the present man from the eye of the people.

Justice *Ranjan Gogoi*, while hearing a public interest litigation (PIL) against the appointment of an IPS officer as the Chief Vigilance Commissioner (CVC), on 11 September 2018, said that the PILs are for the poor. He added that anyone could knock on its doors for justice.

The advocate for the case, *Mr. Prasant Bhusan,* contended that the notification mentioned the age limit of 60 years and the age of the selected man was 62 years. As the law stipulated no age limit, Justice *Gogoi* said that the aggrieved parties should have approached the court as soon as the notification was issued.

The present man knocked at the door of the Supreme Court of India 645 times in 17 years. As it denies freedom, the people are not aware of it. His book on Prime Minister *Mr. Narendra Modi* titled "WE WILL STRANGE YOU" did not reach the mind of even any one citizen of India. The tragedy is that the present man's gift to the English language goes unnoticed. The media mafia thinks that the contribution of the present man to nation building would come to the notice of the people if his contribution to the English language is revealed. The English learners all over the world are affected. It is a human rights problem.

The new Chief Justice of India, *Justice Gogoi,* might use Article 14 or142 or 19 or 39 to establish justice in India.

Justice *Ranjan Gogoi* was, on 13 September 2018, appointed as the 46th Chief Justice of India. President of India *Mr.Ram Nath Kovind,* quickly signed the warrants of appointment and a notification was issued immediately. He will be sworn in as the Chief Justice of India on 3rd October 2018.

Earlier, Chief Justice of India *Dipak Misra* recommended his name for this post. The recommendation indicated that the 'snake' had been killed by the impeachment motion moved by the opposition parties against Chief Justice *Dipak Misra.* The future alone would tell whether this conclusion is right or not.

Apparently, the opinion of the judges of the Supreme Court of India is against any superseding. President of India also might have played a key role.

An advocate, *Mr. Satyaveer Sharma,* along with a *Mr. Luthra,* on 25 September 2018, filed a public interest litigation (PIL) against the appointment saying that Justice *Gogoi* had sabotaged the system through his press conference, Next day, it was rejected by a bench headed by Chief Justice *Misra* because it was too late.

The system punishes the present man in diverse ways. The revelation might lead to greater torture. But, everyone in the system knows that the works of the present man are being concealed from the eye of the right-thinking people.

A punishment to Justice *Ranjan Gogoi might* have sent a very wrong message to the unsuspecting people also.

The present man chose not to send any letter during this time because one should not poke his nose when the things go in the right direction.

Invoking Article 142 of the Constitution of India, a bench of the Supreme Court of India headed by Chief Justice of India *Dipak Misra,* on 14 September 2018, directed the Government of Kerala to give Re.fifty lakh as damages to the former scientist of the Indian Space Research Organization (ISRO), *Mr. Nambinarayanan.* The court described the prosecution against him as a 'malicious' one.

The Article 142 says that the Supreme Court of India, in the exercise of its jurisdiction, may pass such decree or make such order as is necessary for doing 'complete justice' in any cause or matter pending before it.

Based on this Article, the Supreme Court of India can do anything constitutional to establish justice in India.

In this case, it has done something to undo the harm done to a citizen of India. Thus, *Mr. Nambinarayanan* got a consolatory judgement after 24 years in the ISRO-spy case.

Congress President *Mr. Rahul Gandhi,* on 14 September 2018, said that the CBI aided the escape of *Mr. Vijay Mallya* to Britain.

The BJP, on 15 September 2018, said that *Mr. Sonia Gandhi* and *Mr. Rahul Gandhi* had flown free of cost in the Kingfisher Airline (of *Mr. Mallya*).

When the present man said the above, the media did not report it. When the BJP says this, they report it. This indicates the nexus between the ruling class and the BJP.

Congress President *Mr. Rahul Gandhi* appointed former Union Minister *Mr. P. Chithambaram* as the Chairman of the manifesto committee of the 2019 elections.

Earlier he revoked a suspension order against *Mr. Manisankar Iyer.* The developments show that *Mr. Rahul Gandhi* is a prisoner in the hand of the ruling class. He wants to rule India simply as their hired man.

The Union Government, on 17 September 2018, decided to merge three public sector banks – *Dena Bank, Vijaya Bank* and *Bank of Baroda.*

This work shows that it is a bad faith action. So long as the Supreme of India denies freedom, there is no use in repeating everything and the Government can do anything.

Former French President *Mr. Hollande* on 24 September 2018, disclosed that the manufacture of *Rafale* aircraft in India was given to *Mr. Anil Ambani* only at the instance of Prime Minister of India *Mr. Narendra Modi* and that he had no other choice before him. This shows that he no longer wants to be a co-conspirator of *Mr. Modi.*

It must be noted that Prime Minister *Mr. Modi* is dragging even the world leaders to the mud.

The revelation is consistent with the prediction that *Mr. Anil Ambani* summoned Prime Minister *Mr. Modi* to Paris and that the Indian bureaucracy did not negotiate the deal.

Congress President *Mr. Rahul Gandhi,* on 24 September 2018, depicted Prime Minister *Mr. Modi* as the "Commander -in- Thief" of India.

*Mr. Rahul Gandhi* is the leader of the opposition. The Prime Minister must have rebutted the charges levelled against him. But he chose not to give a reply.


The Ministry of Housing and Urban Affairs, on 24 September 2018, demanded *Mrs. Sonia Gandhi* to vacate the *Teen Murthy* complex. She is the Chairperson of the *Jawaharlal Nehru Memorial Fund (JNMF).*

The Government should have simultaneously asked *Mr. Retan Tata* to vacate the *Tata Trust* for converting the *Tata Trust* into a private limited company. This is to enforce rule of law.


The people of *Maldives* elected the leader of the combined opposition parties, *Mr. Ibrahim Mohamed Solih* in the Presidential election. China, apparently, spent a huge amount of money to influence the voters. Yet it failed.

But it could make India its slave nation.


The militant people shot dead an MLA and a former MLA in the *Andra Pradesh State* on 29 September 2018.

The above killings are an outcome of the noninformation of this work to the people.


According to some reports, *Mr. Ratan Tata* is making drastic changes in the *Tata Trust.*

The members of a Charitable Trust cannot be its beneficiaries. If he is a member of the *Tata Trust,* he cannot claim remuneration.

It must be noted that he  is committing one illegality after another.

He usurped the public sector VSNL.

He passed a resolution to convert the *Tata Trust* into a private limited company.

Charitable Trusts should not campaign for political or legal change. But the *Tata Trust* controls the public mind in India.

The President of India need not sanction it, remove its members or take over its property to prevent harm being done. But he should have informed these letters to the people. That did not happen because the *Tata Trust* did not allow it.

According to the media, the *National Museum* in *Kolkata* made some of its possessions accessible online.

In this year, India sent some precious antiques of *Mugal*  era to *Italy*. Some people plundered it. What happened afterwards is not known. *Prime Minister Mr. Narendra Modi* is duty bound to give an answer.

The Union Government, on 26 September 2018, hiked the import duty on 19 items to fetch Re.4000 crore.

Items like toys, utensils could have been included in the prohibited list.

Further, the Government has not addressed the trade deficit of *India* with *China.*

A Supreme Court of India bench headed by Chief Justice *Dipak Misra,* on 27 September 2018, ruled that adultery is no longer a crime. The 158- year old adultery law punished men only. Hereafter, men and women will be equally guilty.

The message of the judgement is that adultery in certain circumstances is consistent with the human nature and that men can live happily without mentioning it to his wife so long as it has no other adverse consequences like conceiving.

Further, the judgement, apparently, removes the distinction between married women and unmarried women.

It is not clear whether it would give relief to *Bishop Franco* or not.

Union Minister *Miss. Uma Bharathi* said that the concept of equal rights is a western concept and that the women have been considered superior to men in India. According to her, if equal rights are given to massive fish and small fish, the former would eat the latter. But CPI (M) leader *Mrs. Brinda Karat,* and other women's leaders welcomed the judgement as women would not be bound by the matrimonial bond.

A report, on 27 September 2018, said that Prime Minister of India *Mr. Narendra Modi* is secretly printing Indian currency notes in China.

What a calamity is this? The present man requested him to recirculate the demonetized currency notes. *Mr. Modi* considered it as a shameful act. Is it not a shame to print Indian currency notes - that too secretly - in China? Is it the meaning of the 'Make in India' policy? He has taken away the jobs of Indians only to give them to the Chinese. The Supreme Court of India abetted it is a different matter.

The USA, on 27 September 2018, told India that it would substitute Iranian oil with its oil.

Now, India cannot come out with any excuse. It will have to agree to the demands of the USA. However, the commission agents might stand in the way.

A bench of the Supreme Court of India, on 28 September 2019, declared that women of all ages could visit the deity at *Sabarimala.*

It is believed that the deity in *Sabarimala* does not want to see women. The belief is not usually questioned even if it is the belief of a deity. All religions preach equality of gender. But women are not allowed in some places of worship by their parent religions. Catholic Christian religion does not ordain women as priests. Will the court do justice?

Further, the court does not enforce the Constitution of India to give freedom to Indians. But in small matters, it talks of equity and creates conflicting situations. It has forfeited its right to exist.

The Chief Justice of India designate, Justice *Ranjan Gogoi*, on 29 September 2018, said, "Just as I construct a house in Assam, the Bar gives new shape and meaning to the words of the statute. You as a lawyer and me as the judge we are responsible for what society is. What we get to see how human rights, political rights, social rights of the 130 crore Indians are delivered"

It is true that every man in India creates his own India. The mind of a judge of the Supreme Court of India has the power to change India. A political leader can also do this. But the manipulators now rule India.

Apparently, Justice *Ranjan Gogoi* accepts responsibility for the denial of political rights to the citizens and for the present totally corrupt condition.

Outgoing Chief Justice of India *Dipak Misra*, on 1 October 2018, addressed the Bar. He said, "Indian judiciary is the strongest one in the world. History can be sometimes kind, and unkind. I don't judge people by their history. But by their activities, perspective. In my whole career as a judge, I never dissociated myself from the lady of equity. I am indebted to Bar at every level and go from here with satisfaction."

If a man lacks in something, he would assert that he possesses it.

The Indian judiciary appears as the strongest one because it remains under the care of the media mafia. However, it will remain strong only when it enforces the essence of the Constitution of India.

But the Indian judiciary destroys the Constitution of India for its wealth and sends small economic offenders like 'conductors' to jail. It rigs the elections by denying freedom. There is no bigger unjust entity anywhere in the world. For the same reason, Chief Justice *Misra* was afraid of light until the last day last minute in office.

In the above function, Justice *Ranjan Gogoi* said that the judges of the Supreme Court of India are committed, and they would remain committed.

The judges of the Supreme Court of India might or might not have taken the plunder. But they have been allowing plunder by denying freedom for the last 17 years.

A committed judge means a judge committed to the Constitution of India. A judge committed to the Constitution of India would not be afraid of light. Therefore, 1300 million people would get freedom to know this work on the 3rd October 2018.

The Union Government, on 1 October 2018, decided to hand over 36 hydrocarbon blocks to the private parties. In this matter, the Supreme Court of India does violence to Article 19. It does this to annihilate Article 39.

*Mr. Nambinarayanan* now says that seven officers of the *Intelligence Bureau (IB)* besides the media were involved in the bad faith action against him. He wants a CBI probe to identify the people responsible for the dissemination of news and views in India.

This is the real tragedy. He thinks that the CBI, Research and Analysis Wing (RAW), Chief Vigilance Commissioner (CVC), National Human Rights Commission (NHRC), Supreme Court of India and even the President of India are different from the IB.

However, due to 24 years of suffering, he perceives that something wrong is going on in India. He comes close to the real culprits, but he is for away.

The men responsible for the non-information of 645 letters to the people are the real culprits. One can put the blame on the IB, CBI, CVC, NHRC, Supreme Court of India, Prime Minister of India, President of India or the Tata Trust.

The Supreme Court of India can do anything under Article 142 to establish justice in India.

However, the President of India is specifically responsible for giving justice to Indians. He can use Article 143 or any other Articles for this. But he does not think that it is expedient on him even to obtain an opinion from the Supreme Court of India.

The present man repeatedly said that the Supreme Court of India can establish justice even if the heavens fall. It need not do anything strange for this but must enforce the law for this. Instead, it misused its office and concealed the letters from the eye of the people.

The real culprits disseminate news and views just to steer the attention of the people to other matters. They do this to plunder the nation. The ISRO-spy case is an example.

The non-information of the letters of the present man to the people led to the privatization of 34 public sector undertakings and the alienation unlimited public resources and public money. The political leaders responsible for this heinous unconstitutional act, pretend like saints.

The noninformation of this work, led to the death of thousands of Sri Lankan Tamils and hundreds of Indian fishermen.

The employees and the people are being divested of their pension because of the non-information of this work to the people.

Had the letters been brought to the notice of the people, Prime Minister *Mr. Modi* might not have given money to the *Reliance Industries Limited (RIL)* in the pretext of gas subsidy. He might not have signed the *Rafale* fighter aircraft deal.

He might not have erected a statue for *Sardar Vallabhbhai Patel* or jeopardized the employment opportunities of the Indians abroad.

Trade is essential for growth. But it shall not be at the cost of fair play. China sells a box containing a hundred pieces as a box containing ten pieces. Thus, it evades taxes. The foreign exchange goes to China through illegal routes. In contrast, India imposes so many taxes on the Indian industries and cripple them. The publication of this work might have prevented this and created jobs in India.

The noninformation of this work leads to the criminalization of Indian politics.

The non-information of this work imparts illegitimacy to the governments. In fact, *Dr. Manmohan Singh* and *Mr. Narendra Modi* might not have become prime ministers. They were imposed on the people by the ruling class. This has the effect of rigging elections.

It affected the chances of a citizen of India to seize power.

The Supreme Court of India keeps these letters as **a dark secret.** All chief justices since June 2001 are involved in it. This enabled the media to deprive the people of their life, liberty and property without the due process of law.

Plato says, **"We can easily forgive a child who is afraid of dark, the real tragedy of life is when men are afraid  of the light".**

**2**

# What makes the nation great?

As soon as *Justice Ranjan Gogoi* assumed charge as the Chief Justice of India, a retired Judge of the Supreme Court of India, *N. Santosh Hedge*, advised him "to give an impression that the judges are one when it comes to justice."

*Justice Hedge* did not reveal the existence of this work to the people till his last day last minute in office. He expects *Chief Justice Gogoi* to keep this work away from the watchful eye of the people. Therefore, he says that all judges must be one in disqualifying this work.

On 3 October 2018, advocate *Prasant Bhusan* mentioned a case before *Chief Justice Ranjan Gogoi*. The Chief Justice retorted, "No urgent mentioning of cases will be allowed till parameters are worked out. When someone is to be hanged tomorrow, then we can understand. If someone is being released today, then yes. If someone being evicted today, then yes."

The urgent mentioning has been reserved for a few advocates like him. They never mention the key points to enlighten the judges or the people. They score same side goal in all key cases. One day, advocate *Mathews J. Nedumpara* appeared for *Justice Karman*. He did not mention the key legal point and the victim did not get any relief.

. But the people have a very high opinion about advocates like *Mr. Prasant Bhusan*. 'He is a bold advocate. See, he alone points out his fingers at *Mr. Mukesh Ambani* and *Mr. Tata*. He serves the nation very well' This is the opinion of the people about *Mr. Prasant Bhusan*.

But *Mr. Prasant Bhusan* never mentioned Article 39 or the Article 19 to the judges till date. He has not mentioned the word 'freedom' to the judges He tirelessly denies freedom to conserve the illegally acquired assets of the *Reliance Industries Limited (RIL)* and the *Tata Trust*.

Therefore, the parameters to be framed must be to reserve at least one chance to every advocate, say, in one month.

Advocate *ML Sharma* filed a public interest litigation petition in the Supreme Court of India on 4 October 2018. The petition sought an independent probe into the *Rafale fighter jet deal*. A similar petition was filed by a leader of the Congress Party, *Mr. Tebseen Poonavalla*, on the same day. The bench said that the petitions were grossly inadequate. It said that it was not considering the allegation of corruption in the deal or the pricing or the suitability of the aircraft made in the petition. Instead, the bench asked the Government to furnish, in a sealed cover, the decision-making process by 29 October 2018 and decided to hear the case on 1 November 2018. The bench said that it wanted to be satisfied about the legitimacy of the decision-making process.

The above direction of the bench came to the notice of a negligible section of the educated people. **They welcomed the above direction of the bench with folded hands. They thought that India got an ingenuous chief justice for the first time.**

Now, former Solicitor General of India *Mr.Ranjit Kumar* approached the Supreme Court of India with another Public Interest Litigation (PIL). He wanted the Supreme Court of India to lay down some new guidelines for the PILs. He said, "One CPIL, one common cause or one *ML Sharma* come to this court in a PIL representing the whole country. And a sweeping order is passed. These orders will have ramifications of several parties who have not even been heard by the court. These orders and judgements affect license holders. But they are not even issued notices"

"Do you want a review of these judgements?" The Chief Justice asked.

"No, my lord. I am requesting you to lay down some guidelines now".

"Sorry, we are not going to do that"

The above reply of the Chief Justice of India gave the impression that he wanted to do justice in the *Rafale deal.*

Editor of The Print *Mr. Sekar Gupta* on 11 October 2018, said that notwithstanding the controversies, the *Rafale* aircraft would fly in the Indian skies and Indians would be proud of it.

This gave the impression that the ruling class had a secret understanding with the Chief Justice of India to give a green signal to the *Rafale deal* after a shadow fighting. Thus, the people began to smell a conspiracy in the case.

The reason for the suspicion is that the bench suppressed the consequences of the Article 39 from the people.

In contrast, some others considered his comments as a challenge of the ruling class to the Supreme Court of India.

However, the intergovernmental agreements would never make Article 39 an invalid one.

The Congress Party, on 15 October 2018, said Prime Minister of India *Mr. Narendra Modi* was directly involved in the *Rafale deal* and that he had much to hide about it. The Chief Justice of India rejected it as politics.

The President of Sri Lanka, *Mr. Maithripala Sirisena,* on 16 October 2018, told his Cabinet that an Indian Intelligence Agency, *Research and Analysis Wing (RAW),* was plotting to kill him. He added that it might have happened without the knowledge of Prime Minister of India *Mr. Narendra Modi.* A *Mr. Thomas* hailing from Kerala was arrested by Sri Lanka presumably because he knew the plot. The Hindu reported this on 16 October 2018.

India did not react to his statement.

The Directorate of Enforcement, on 19 October filed four cases under the Prevention of Money Laundering Act (PMLA) for criminal conspiracy, cheating and corruption. Two cases pertain to the merger of the Air India (AI) and the Indian Airlines (IA) and the alleged corruption in the purchase of 116 aircraft (48 from Airbus and 68 from the Boeing) for Re.70,000 crore in 2005-2006 by the UPA Government, leasing many aircraft and ceding of profit making routes and timings to domestic and international airlines. The cases had been filed following a secret direction from the Supreme Court of India on a petition filed by the Centre for Public Interest Litigation (CPIL).

Thus, the UPA Government handed over benefits worth Re.35000 crore to its promoters in the above deals. The court did not deem it necessary to attach the assets of the beneficiaries or to enforce Article 19. Now the employees are being asked to pay for it.

Congress President *Mr.Rahul Gandhi,* on 13 October 2018, met the employees of the public-sector Hindustan Aeronautic Limited (HAL) at Bangalore. He told them that *Rafale* was their right. He attacked Prime Minister *Mr. Narendra Modi* for the *Rafale deal.*

He should have gone to the Mumbai and Delhi airports to meet the employees. He forgot that he gifted them to the ruling class.

If he comes to power, he would hand over the HAL to them depicting it as a loss-making unit.

He did not restore the 34 Public Sector Undertakings (PSUs) alienated by the NDA Government.

Now he wants to face the 2019 election flanked by *Mr. P. Chithambaram* and *Dr. Manmohan Singh.*

As there is no freedom, he can do anything.


"The Finance Ministry finds future disinvestment road slippery" This was the heading of the news item in the Indian Express on 21 October 2018.

The Indian Express is running the nation. It can take anything.


The Times of India, on 21 October 2018, reported that the CBI helped *Mr. Sivasankaran* to escape from India.  He had removed Re.600 crore from the IDBI Bank. The Prime Minister of India *Mr. Narendra Modi* and the Supreme Court of India did not do anything after the revelation.


The CBI, on 21 October 2018, raided its own office and booked the Special Director, *Mr. Rakesh Asthana* and No.2 in the CBI for a bribery of Re.2 crore. The case involves businessman *Moin Qureshi.*

The Chief Vigilance Commissioner (CVC) on 22 October 2018, directed the Prime Minister's Office (PMO) to disclose the complaints of corruption received against the union ministers since 2014 and the action taken on them as well as to share the information on the quantum and the value of black money brought back from abroad since *Mr. Narendra Modi* came to power.

The Government ignored the direction. The Chief Justice of India stood by the Government.

CBI Special Director *Mr. Asthana* wrote to the Chief Vigilance Commissioner (CVC) that the CBI Director *Mr. Alok Varma* took a bribe of Re.2 crore from a *Mr. Satis Babu Sana* in connection with the *Moin Qureshi* case. After a preliminary enquiry, the CVC served a notice on 11 September 2018 to *Mr. Alok Varma.* The people suspected a high-level conspiracy involving the Chief Justice of India and the Prime Minister of India in the complaint. Otherwise, no human being might have dared to file a false complaint like this particularly after being booked by his own organization.

*Mr. Alok Varma* described the complaint as a desperate attempt of a tainted person to discredit the officers. He, further, questioned the integrity of *Mr. Asthana.* He added that the CBI was investigating his role in at least half a dozen cases.

On 22 October 2018, the CBI raided its own office and arrested Deputy Superintendent of Police *Mr. Devendra Kumar* for forging a recorded statement of *Mr. Sathis Sena* against *Mr. Alok Varma.* His house also was raided. He was produced before the magistrate. The CBI said that he was running an extortion racket in the name of investigation.

On 24 October 2018, the Government of India – based on the recommendation of the CVC -sent Director Varma and Special Director *Asthana* on indefinite leave and posted *Mr. Nageswar Rao I.P.S.,* as an acting director. As there is no freedom, the people felt that the Prime Minister had enlisted the support of the Chief Justice of India for this.

*Mr. Alok Varma* went to Supreme Court of India.

Advocate *Mr. Prasant Bhusan* appeared for *Mr. Alok Varma* and argued that he, along with *Mr. Arun Shourie* and *Yaswant Sinha* had submitted a petition to *Mr. Alok Varma* to probe the *Rafale* deal. The Union Government removed him only to prevent him from probing the *Rafale* deal.

*Mr. Subramonia Swamy* described the procedure followed by the Government to remove the director as a flawed one.

*Mr. Alok Varma* contended that *Mr. Ashana* obstructed several investigations and concocted evidences to implicate him in corruption cases. He sought his own reinstatement saying that he could be removed by the appointing authority only -namely the selection panel comprising Chief Justice of India, Prime Minister of India and the leader of the opposition.

*Mr. Sekhar Gupta,* on 24 October 2018, said that no one would be ultimately found guilty. This conveyed the impression that the Supreme Court of India is enacting a drama with his knowledge.

A Bench of the Supreme Court of India comprising *Chief Justice Ranjan Gogoi* and *justices K.M. Joseph and S.K. Kaul* heard the case on 26 October 2018.

Advocates *Mr. Prasant Bhusam* and *Mr.Nariman* demanded the reinstatement of *Mr. Alok Varma.*

The bench -in an interim order- said:

1. The enquiry in respect of the allegations made in the letter of the Cabinet Secretary on 24 October 2018 about the present CBI Director,

*Mr. Alok Varma* must be completed by the CVC within two weeks under the supervision of the retired Chief Justice of India, *A.K. Patnaik.*

2. The mass transfers of the CBI officers ordered by the interim Director, *Mr. Nageswara Rao,* would be scrutinized by the court.

The charges against Special Director *Mr. Asthana* would not be dropped

4. The new director should not take any policy decision

5.All decisions taken by him after assuming power must be submitted to the court in a sealed cover and

6. This order is a one -time exception in view of the peculiar situation prevailing in the CBI.

The probe supervision is a huge blow to the Government. To proceed against *Mr. Asthana*, the Chief Justice wanted to be doubly sure that *Mr. Alok Varma* did not take any money from anyone in any case.

*Dr. Manmohan Singh,* former Prime Minister of India, on 27 October 2018, described *Mr. Narendra Modi* as a paradoxical prime minister who failed electorate. The people hear his words because he is a hired man of the ruling class.


The Income Tax Department raided hundreds of locations of the V.V. Minerals on 25 October 2018. The Article 39 demands not raids but the take-over of all minerals.

There are reports that about 500 acre of city-land belonging to *Mr.Paneerdhas* was taken over by the Government of Tamil Nadu citing the Land Ceiling Act.

The fact that he failed to bring his land under the Company Act, should not have been the reason for the take-over.

The militant people killed five soldiers in the Chhattisgarh State on 27 October 2018.

*Justice Chelmeswar,* on 28 October 2018, said, "I cannot disclose the reason for the press conference now". The people now think that the press conference was a conspiracy to deny freedom to Indians. Many people think that they simply hoodwinked the people. Otherwise, the people might have seen freedom the moment the present Chief Justice took charge,

Senior CBI officer *Mr.A.K. Basu* moved the Supreme Court of India on 30 October 2018, stating that he had incriminating evidence against Special CBI director *Mr. Rakesh Asthana.* He submitted that his transfer to Port Blair was not in public interest but in private interest. The court was not inclined to take immediate action but said that it would take necessary action in due course. in view of the CVC probe against CBI Director *Mr. Alok Varma.*

The Chief Justice of India is the most powerful person in India. His accountability, therefore, must be the greatest. He has the responsibility to ensure rule of law. It is not easy for the ordinary people. Natural judges are necessary for this. He should have immediately asked Mr. Basu to file an affidavit in the matter.

But, he also is a human being. He might have his own interests. Perhaps, he did not want to become the odd man to go out of the system.

The Supreme Court of India, on 30 October 2018, refused to hear the Ayodhya case. It said that it had other priorities.

Some parties want to show that the Supreme Court of India is against a religion. They want to play a victim card. The Chief Justice of India refused to fall into their trap.

The *Rafale* issue came to the court on 1 November 2018. The court wanted to know the details of pricing. The advocate for the Government refused saying it as a classified matter. The counsel said that the Government did not share this information with the Parliament. The previous Governments did not share the information with the court.

The court said that it wanted to know the constitutionality of the decision making. It wanted the Government to give the reply in an affidavit within ten days.

The people felt that the Chief Justice wanted to do justice in this matter. The present man thought that he would not hesitate to give freedom.

Deputy Superintendent of Police of the CBI *Mr.Ajay Kumar Basi,* on 1 November 2018, informed the Supreme Court of India, that the agency had intercepted a conversation between RAW's *Goel,* Head of the RAW's West Asia Operations. and banker *Somesh Prasad,* a suspect in a bribery investigation warning him not to return to India at any cost.

The complaint showed that the RAW, Intelligence Bureau (IB) and the CBI had the habit of reporting many serious pieces of information to the manipulators before reporting to the Government. Therefore, the Chief Justice of India should have asked the competent authority to take necessary action after declaring freedom to Indians. But he ignored it. This gave a bad message to the people.

*Mr. G.N. Bajpai,* former chairman of Life Insurance Corporation of India (LIC) and Securities and Exchange Board of India (SEBI) resigned from the newly constituted Board of Infrastructure Leasing & Financial Services (IL&FS) citing personal reasons, The media said that he was under the scanner of Serious Frauds Investigation Office (SFIO). He was an independent director on the Kingfisher Board and Multi Commodity Exchange (MCX) of India.

Why did the LIC put money in the IL&FS? The case is like the "Satyam case". In this matter also, the Chief Justice should have issued direction to confiscate the assets of the beneficiaries after declaring freedom to Indians.

The present man had given a solution for it.

*Justice Chelameswar,* on 3 November 2018, said that he was happy to be remembered as a good judge than a bad chief justice.

The greater the responsibility, the greater the risk associated with it. When the chief justice tends to cover up something serious, he becomes not a bad man but a criminal.

Congress President Mr. Rahul Gandhi, on 10 November 2018, said that Prime Minister of India *Mr. Narendra Modi* waived loans worth Re.3.5 lakh crore of 15 select industrialists during his tenure. He added that the Congress Party would recover it and give it to the tribal people, youth, farmers and poor women.

His Government also had given similar amounts.

The Union Government wanted the Reserve Bank of India (RBI) to hand over about 3.5 lakh crore to the Government for public investments. To this, former Union Minister Mr. P. Chithambaram said that the act of laying hands on the reserves of the RBI would have catastrophic consequences. He asked the Government to tell the reason why it remained silent for the last four and a half years.

His statement shows that he has not read the last few letters submitted to the President of India.

Solemn ceremonies took place around the world on 11 November 2018, to mark 100 years to the day since the Armistice that saw the end of World War I.

French President Emmanuel Macron led the International Armistice Day commemorations by the Tomb of the Unknown Soldier that lies at the foot of the Arc de Triomphe monument in Paris.

Mr. Marcon said, "Patriotism is the exact opposite of Nationalism. Nationalism is a betrayal of patriotism. By saying our interests first, who cares about others, we erase what a nation holds dearest, **what gives it life, what makes it great,** and what is essential its moral values. I know that there are old demons which are coming back to the surface. They are ready to wreck chaos and death".

The present man has not listened to a better speech. The French system must be commended for bringing him to the surface.

US President Donald Trump, German Chancellor Angela Merkel, Russian President Vladimir Putin and 67 other world leaders attended the function at Paris. India was represented by Vice President Mr. Venkaiya Naidu. Prime Minister of India Mr. Narendra Modi was conspicuous by his absence. This conveyed the impression that the world leaders are very reluctant to accept him.

The Union Government, on 12 November 2018, filed an affidavit to the Supreme Court of India and submitted the price details of the Rafale deal in a sealed cover. The media, on the same day, disclosed the decision-making process submitted by the Government to the court. It indicated that the Union Cabinet did not take any decision.

According to the affidavit, a negotiation team had been constituted. The team comprising some IAF officers negotiated with the French side for about one year and the approval of the Cabinet Committee on Security was obtained. The offset details were negotiated by a bureaucrat – a confidant of the Prime Minister of India.

The presentation showed that the Rafale aircraft had been selected long before the constitution of the negotiation team.

Further, the approval of the Union Cabinet was not obtained. The message conveyed was that Prime Minister Mr. Modi could not trust the ministers in the Union Cabinet.

However, a part cannot play the role of the whole. The deal was out and out an unconstitutional one.

The message of the offset policy is as follows. "I did not give any money to *Mr. Anil Ambani* or others. I gave Re.30,000 crore from the treasury to the French company only. It is my pleasure to load my promoters like this. I can give Re three lakh crore or Re. thirty lakh crore to my promoters. This is for the prosperity of India. If *Mr. Vajpayee* could hand over 34 PSUs to his promoters, I can give this to my promoters. *Dr. Manmohan Singh* shared the revenue secretly. Hereafter, the revenue of the nation is to be shared openly with *Mr. Anil Ambani* like people.

When I gave Re.59000 crore to *Mr. Mukesh Ambani* and others, the Supreme Court of India supported me. *Justice Gogoi* became the Chief Justice of India only because of the ruling class. He will never point out Article 39 or Article 19 to the people. In this way, he would make India *great*".

CBI Director *Mr. Alok Varma* on, 16 November 2018, told the Supreme Court of India that *Mr. Rakesh Asthana*, Prime Minister's Office (PMO) and *Mr. Sushil Modi* worked together to book *Mr. Lalu Prasad Yadav*. He disclosed that an official of the PMO asked him to pursue a case against *Mr. Lalu Prasad Yadav* in the Railway catering case. He added that he would disclose the name if the court is ready to take necessary action.

The bench headed by the Chief Justice did not entertain it. This makes the officers in the PMO clean.

The CVC handed over the enquiry report on the allegations against CBI Director *Mr. Alok Varma* on 16 November 2018.

Justice A.K. Patnaik supervised the CVC enquiry. He submitted his 50-page report to the Chief Justice of India. The Chief Justice expressed his gratitude to Justice Patnaik.

Everyone thought that Mr. Alok Varma would be either sent to jail or reinstated forthwith.

*Mr. Sekar Gupta,* Editor -in- Chief of the Print, on 14 November 2018, said that the stand taken by the Supreme Court of India, weakened the executive. He added that the assertion of the court that it was a onetime exception is not a correct one. He warned the court not to do it again.

Thus, he says that he would put to death all judges if they tend to repeat what they did or even tell the truth.

What is going on is an organized plunder. The Chief Justice of India functions as an odd man and that he would be ignored if he dares to do it again. This is the message of his speech. It must be noted that earlier, on 24 October 2018, he said no one would be found guilty.

*Mr. N. Ram,* Chairman of the Hindu Publishing Group, on 16 November 2018, received the Raja Ram Mohan Roy Award for Excellence in Journalism. He had, along with *Mr. Sekar Gupta* threatened to eliminate the present man. He got the award due to the noninformation of this work to the people.

The Union Government and the Reserve bank of India, on 19 November 2018, decided to set up a committee to apportion the surplus fund of the RBI. The RBI must surrender the money extracted for imports to the Government. The present developments show that the foreign exchange reserves of India is being siphoned off in an illegal way.

An officer of the CBI, Mr. MK Sinha on 19 November 2018, submitted before the Supreme Court of India that Central Vigilance Commissioner (CVC) Mr. K.V. Chowdary. Union Minister Mr. Haribhai Parthibhai Chowdary, National Security Adviser Mr. Ajit Doval and an officer in the Prime Minister's Office were either receiving huge amount of money or were interfering in various cases every day.

Mr. Alok Verma said that Mr. Asthana was under probe accepting a bribe of Re.3 crore from a Mr. Satish Sena. He added that tainted officers were appointed in the CBI.

The Supreme Court of India, on 19 November 2018, refused to hear Mr. Alok Varma and adjourned the case to 29 November 2018. The Chief Justice of India said that the reply of Mr. Alok Varma had been leaked to media before submitting to him.

The media reports showed that Mr. Alok Varma did not take money from anyone as alleged by Mr. Asthana. The moment the Chief Justice noticed it, he adjourned the case.

The Chief Justice of India should have either put him to death or given him liberty. It is true that he might over-throw the system. If rule of law demands this, the Chief Justice of India need not be worried about it. Now, everything would recoil on the Chief Justice of India. It is not good to the nation.

This is letter No. 647.

Despite the last letter, the Chief Justice of India used his freedom to deny freedom to Indians.

He must release this letter to the media even if it would make him uneasy. He must prove that he has nothing to hide. He must examine **"what makes the nation great"**

# 3

# Give life to the nation

There are reports that the cyclone victims in the Tamil Nadu State did not get what the Gujarat earthquake victims and the Kerala flood victims got. The Supreme Court of India must tell the Prime Minister of India not secretly but through the media that this discrimination must disappear.

Prime Minister of India *Mr. Narendra Modi* on 24 November 2018, said that the Congress Party was scaring the judges of the Supreme Court of India on the grounds of their numbers in the Upper House.

The judges might have told him that they were afraid of the Congress Party in the *Alok Varma* case. Or, he thinks that the Supreme Court of India would reinstate *Mr. Alok Varma* as the director of the Central Bureau of Investigation (CBI)

The *NGO Sherpa,* a French anti-corruption NGO, filed a complaint alleging "potential acts of corruption, granting of undue advantages, influence peddling, complicity of these offences and money laundering by the Government of France and the Dassault Aviation." It is based on the complaint filed by former Indian Union Ministers - *Mr. Arun Shourie* and *Mr.Yaswant Sinha* and advocate *Mr. Prasant Bhusan* mentioning 'abuse of authority and grant of undue advantages to the Central Bureau of Investigation (CBI).". The Indian media reported this on 24 November 2018.

It is pertinent to recall that in deference to the first letter dated 1-6-2001, the then Prime Minister of India, *Mr. A.B. Vajpayee,* wanted to use the public money for public investments. But, *Mr. Arun Shourie* defied it and exhorted the bureaucracy to pick up courage to overrule such letters on file. The then Finance Minister, *Mr. Yashwant Sinha,* opposed a massive public investment programme. He added that "if the privatization process is stopped in the midway, the tiger would eat us"

During this time, advocate *Mr. Prasant Bhusan* did not point out the consequences of Article 39 or the Article 19 to the judges or to the people.

Thus, disqualifying this work, they alienated one Public Sector Undertaking (PSU) after another. The Tata Trust bought the public sector VSNL against public money. The IPCL and the HZL were sold to the charge sheeted companies in violation of the guidelines devised for privatization. The above three men were the important beneficiaries. There were reports that some present Union Ministers – son of *Mr.Yashwant Sinha* included - had money in Paradise and they wanted to buy the Air India.

The media and the entire world now commend them as anti-corruption crusaders!

Thus, the media and the Supreme Court of India project the most corrupt men as the anticorruption crusaders so that the people would vote for them.

Earlier, one day, the Supreme Court of India cancelled the petrol outlets granted by the Members of Parliament. Next day, it allowed the Reliance Industries Limited (RIL) to start petrol outlets all over India. When it was pointed out to the Supreme Court, the RIL shut down some petrol outlets as a show. When it became certain that this work would never come out, the RIL resumed the petrol outlet business all over India.

During critical phases, the letters were sent to the TV channels and the newspapers all over the world. But they did not write or utter a word regarding this work.

If a letter is sent to the, say, *Thanthi TV,* its editor and a few others would go through it and then they would disqualify it. They might use it to enrich their knowledge but would never reveal the source of their knowledge to the people. They simply think that it is their privilege to receive letters from the people only to be concealed by them

Likewise, the President of India would share the letter with the Prime Minister of India and some others including the media personnel.

Even the successive Chief Justices of India might have shared the information with their colleagues and the media with the wink that it should not be informed to the people. "It is an organized crime. You are an odd man. So, you are out of the system. We cannot but follow the odd-man out policy. You try to own a TV channel to propagate your views" This is their reply.

The newspapers and the TV channels all over the world, all judges of the High Courts in India, all prominent political leaders all over India and the State Governments also give the same reply.

Now, the above conclusion is true even with the blogs.

Further, even if the Supreme Court of India takes a decision to enforce freedom of expression and release all letters to the media, the people would not know the good fortune.

This has disastrous consequences.

If the Chief Justice of India is ready to inform this work to the people, CBI Director *Mr. Alok Varma* and his team would get liberty before 29 November 2018 and they would be free to act as per the demands of the Constitution of India. They would succeed in even enforcing freedom of expression.

If he is not ready to inform the letters to the people, *Mr. Alok Varma* would be sent out of the system based on the odd-man -out policy,

Unanimous decision is a characteristic feature of democracy. In India, the political leaders, law enforcement agencies, Supreme Court of India and the media have jointly decided to plunder the nation under one principle or other. The savage weapon in their hand is denial of freedom of expression. Some leaders might go to jail. Even then they would not say that the Indians are being denied freedom.

During such situations, the Chief Justice of India should stand erect and point out the salient features of the Constitution to correct the system. This is the purpose of the Constitution. But the Chief of India is not ready to do this for the last 17 years. One or two chief justices might have tried their level best to give freedom, but they failed and allowed the system to die.

*Union Finance Minister Mr. Arun Jaitely*, on 24 November 2018, said, "It is a question of the credibility of the court. We are accountable to the people not the court. The people must speak so that it would become a reference point"

The CBI concealed hundreds of letters. However, *Mr. Alok Varma* tried to give some credibility to the CBI by preventing as many offences as possible. Now the people think that even if the Supreme Court of India wants to do something good to the CBI, it would be with a screw. If the CBI promotes corruption, the court would not interfere. If it prevents corruption, it would interfere. This gives the impression that the court exists only to pervert justice. Thus, the Supreme Court of India is fast losing its credibility even in the eye of *Union Minister Mr. Arun Jaitely.*

646 letters sent in 17 years are being buried in the Supreme Court of India. The present Chief Justice buried two letters.

*Union Minister Mr. Arun Jaitely* says that the letters should become a reference point. But, the present Chief Justice of India revels in concealing the letters from the people.

The Chief Justice received the letters by his position. Had he been an ordinary man from Assam, the present man might not have written to him.

He is not incapable of reading aright the Indian situation. **He must use his talents to *give life the nation.***

# 4

# A slave

The Constitution Day is celebrated on November 26. The Chief Justice of India hosted a dinner on the penultimate day. The Prime Minister of India and the Vice President of India attended the dinner.

Addressing an inaugural function organized in connection with the Constitution Day today, *Chief Justice of India Ranjan Gogoi said, "The Constitution is the voice of the marginalized as well as the prudence of the majority and continues to be a guide in moments of crisis and uncertainty. It is in our best interest to heed the advice of the Constitution. If we do not, our hubris will result in sharp descent into chaos.*

*When the Constitution was brought into force, it was widely criticized. But time has weakened the criticism and it is a matter of immense pride that it has been referred to with vigor in the last several decades. It is not a document frozen in time and today is not an occasion to celebrate but to test constitutional promises. Are we Indians live under the conditions of freedom, equality and dignity? These are questions that I ask myself. Undoubtedly great advances have been made but there is a lot left to be done. Today we need not just celebration but also to chalk out a roadmap for the future"*

He said the above after freezing 647 letters and the *Alok Varma case.*

The Supreme Court of India did not heed the advice of the Constitution for over 17 years. After listening to the speech of *Chief Justice Gogoi* the people think that he will have to overcome many difficulties to make the Constitution of India a valid one. Does he want to test his promises? Does he admit defeat in the hands of the ruling class?

It must be recalled that four senior most judges of the Supreme Court of India, on January 12, 2018, mounted a revolt against the then Chief Justice of India, *Mr.Dipak Misra,* saying that democracy in India was in danger. They said that many things that were less than desirable were happening in the Supreme Court of India and "unless that institution is saved, democracy would not survive".

Chief Justice of India *Mr. Ranjan Gogoi* was one of the four judges. Everyone thought that he would serve his country with his judgement, if he happened to be the Chief Justice of India.

He knew that the public opinion being manufactured in India belongs to the people sitting away from the scene of action and that the media does not report the facts. He knew that they simply report the views of the plunderers of public property alone.

645 letters were sent to the predecessors of the present Chief Justice of India. They discussed them with various caucuses but never let the people to know them. Some might have released the letters to the media. The media might have disqualified them. They might have made some valiant attempts to enforce freedom of expression. Whatever happened, they failed

As a lover of freedom, the people thought that the present Chief Justice of India would inform the complaints against the judges to the people. He did not do so. He did not inform the public the three letters he received from the present man. **This conveys the impression that he is a slave of the same caucuses.**

The people judge others not based on their actions but based on their reactions. The reaction of the Chief Justice of India to the reply of CBI Director *Mr. Alok Varama* shows that he has no fear about the public opinion that is manufactured by the ruling class.

Therefore, he must show this letter to the people today (26-11-2018) and judge *Mr. Alok Varma* tomorrow.

# 5

# Obstruction of justice

A function was organized in connection with the Constitution Day on 26 November 2018. The Chief Justice India, the judges of the Supreme Court of India, President of India, Prime Minister of India and many others attended the function. On that occasion, *Law Minister Mr. Ravi Sankar Prasad* said, *"Governance is executive's domain. Judiciary must decide how far it can go in taking overpower. Governance is a highly complicated exercise. There are lots of complicated interests, a lot complicated claims, lot of other vested interests that need to be understood when running a government. Mere temptation should not lead to taking over of the power that leads to a larger narrative of some reflection"*

It is not easy to decipher the above words although the message is that the Chief Justice of India should not grant freedom to Indians. However, anyone can tell the meaning of his following words.

*"We can unseat any political leader or political party howsoever popular, howsoever powerful in Delhi or in states"*

The above statement is not a correct one. There is no difference between the leaders of the ruling parties and the opposition parties. All are functioning as the hired men of the plunderers of public property. No leader is ready to even use the word 'freedom'

On that occasion, quoting *John Sturt Mill*, Chief Justice of India *Ranjan Gogoi* said, *"Don't lay your liberties at the feet of even a great man."*

The message of the Chief Justice of India is that the Indians must lay their liberties at the feet of the Chief Justice of India like him. This is the reason why he uses his freedom to deny freedom.

A three - member bench headed by the Chief Justice of India resumed hearing the Central Bureau of Investigation (CBI) Director *Mr. Alok Varma* case on 29 November 2018.

The Solicitor General said that the Government divested of his power in public interest. The message was that *Mr. Alok Varma* tried to prosecute Prime Minister of India *Mr. Narendra Modi* and it was against public interest.

As the bench accepted the above contention, it adjourned the case to December 5, 2018. The Chief Justice India could have put to death *Mr. Alok Varma* or given him liberty.

Usually, a judge hesitates to do injustice when someone tells him that he is going to do injustice. Now the adjournment is **obstruction of justice.** He can drag the case easily until the retirement of *Mr. Alok Varma.* The Chief Justice would say, '**What is morally wrong can be legally right'**

As the Chief Justice of India conceals this work, he can do anything.

The reason for the above conclusion is that the Supreme Court of India can reinstate anyone appointed by anyone at any time. The court need not spend its time on silly arguments.

*Justice Kurian Joseph*, a judge of the Supreme Court of India retired from service today (29-11-2018).

As a judge of the Supreme Court of India, he did not use his freedom to give freedom to Indians. Neither could he bring out the truth nor could he do justice to his profession."

# 6

# The greatest complaint

The Supreme Court of India, on 30 November 2018, directed *Mr. Anil Ambani's* Reliance Communication to give a corporate guarantee of Re. 1400 crore against Re.2900 crore demanded by the Department of Telecommunication for clearing a deal with *Mukesh Ambani*'s Reliance Jio.

The above judgement is an unconstitutional one and an act of corruption.

A section of the Article 39 of the Constitution of India demands that all-natural resources must remain with the Government. Another section of the same Article says that the state shall not load anyone with disproportionate riches at the expense of others.

The Article 39 gives the people a right over the natural assets. The Supreme Court of India must note that this right was in existence even before the formation of the Supreme Court of India, Constitution of India and the political institutions. Therefore, it is a Natural Law that limits the power of the Supreme Court of India and the Parliament.

The Chief Justice of India must note that the people remain under the Indian Union only for the preservation of their property. If the people of Assam have no right over the natural assets, they need not remain under Indian Union at all.

But a man from Assam, functioning as the Chief Justice of India helps alienate the natural assets!

In fact, the Supreme Court of India has been **doing violence against the Article 39** by allowing the Government to alienate the natural resources for the last 17 years with greater intensity than before.

The Supreme Court of India works under the order and direction of the big miners and the High Courts in India work under the state-level miners.

Now, the big miners control the public mind in India and the small miners control the public thought in the state level.

A few years in power is enough to mint a huge amount of money. For this, licenses are being given to the friends and relatives of the political leaders. The recipients manage the election expenses producing rigged results.

To perpetrate the unconstitutional plunder, the Chief Justice of India keeps the salient features of this work away from the eye of the people. **Thus, he does violence against Article 19 This is the greatest complaint against the Chief Justice of India.**

The Chief Justice of India knows whether he has the power to conceal this work from the eye of the people or not.

# 7

# An informed citizenry

*Prime Minister of India Mr. Narendra Modi* attended the G20 summit held on 30 November and 1 December 2018 at Buenos Aires in Argentina. It was the thirteenth meeting of the Group of Twenty (G20). *Mr. Modi* appeared closer to *President Xi Jinping* of China than all others.

A day after demitting office, the reporters approached  former Supreme Court of India judge *Kurian Joseph* and asked him whether he regretted over going public along with justices *Chelameswar, Ranjan Gogoi* and *Madan B. Lokur* against the manner of functioning of the then Chief Justice of India, *Dipak Misra. Justice Kurian Joseph* said, *"I don't regret. It was done consciously as there was no option available.  There were no other options. The press conference was not against any individual but to raise concern on system crisis in the administrative functioning of the Supreme Court of India. **I cannot say the crisis is over"**.* To another question he said. *"There was no political pressure or interference in the discharge of my duties as a judge."*

What crisis does he mean?

The Supreme Court of India acts contrary to the trust reposed in it by the people. It has been mistreating the people for the last 17 years. This may be the reason for the crisis. According to him, *Chief Justice of India Ranjan Gogoi* did not solve the problem.

However, he said that there was no pressure over him. Then why did he not use his freedom to give freedom to Indians? Did he think that freedom is dangerous to Indians? Or, is he not aware of the fact that the Indians have no freedom?

A five-judge bench of the Supreme Court of India headed by *Chief Justice Ranjan Gogoi,* on 1 December 2018, dismissed a petition seeking a review of its 2015 verdict that struck down the National Judicial Appointment Commission Act (NJAC). The bench cited two reasons:1. A delay of 470 days and 2. There was no merit in it.

The petition was filed by National Lawyers Campaign for Judicial Transparency and Reforms.

The judgement is a flawed one because of the following reasons.

1. There is no caste-wise or state-wise reservation of seats.
2. The promotion is not based on date of birth seniority.
3. The selection is not based on any established standing laws.
4. The judges selected by the present system do violence to the Constitution of India and are not capable of enforcing freedom of expression

Evidently, a different breed of judges must reign the Supreme Court of India. Then they would seek the welfare of all citizens and not a part of citizens.

Former Union Minister Aswin Kumar, on 1 December 2018, filed a petition in the Supreme Court of India seeking old age pension to all. He said that he failed as a minister and that he did not want to fail as a citizen.

It became a news for the people all over India.

The present man submitted hundreds of petitions before the Supreme Court of India for the same. But the people did not hear anything about it.

If ten people say that someone is an important man, the media report him to the people. On the contrary, if the ten people say that someone is not important, the media would not report him.

The court simply believes that the present man must be led by the ten men.

In this situation, *Chief Justice of India Ranjan Gogoi* is called upon to do his duty. His duty is to inform the people the letters he receives by his position. His predecessors buried 645 letters of the present man alone in the Supreme Court of India. Chief Justice Gogoi went through five more letters, shared with a few and buried them. Even if there are many others like the present man, the people have a right to know them.

This work is a highly specialized contribution to society. It is complementary to the present knowledge about Indian politics that would create **an informed citizenry.** But, to the eye of the Chief Justice of India, the present man is less important than all other political leaders in India, or he thinks that the present man would overthrow the system to the detriment of 1000 million people.

The truth is that the people would draw strength for the task today.

# 8

# An intelligent answer

Former Union Minister *Mr. Ahmed Patel* today described Emergency as a dark phase in the history of India. It must be noted that he was a Union Minister at that time.

His statement is not a correct one. Anyone going through this work would tell that the period since June 1, 2001is the dark phase in the history of India.

The recently retired Supreme Court of India judge *Justice Kurian Joseph* said that ***former Chief Justice of India Dipak Misra* was remotely controlled** and that he could not say that the present Chief Justice of India is free from the same. He expressed the hope that the things might improve.

**He suspects the integrity of the present Chief Justice of India.** This indicates that the judges of the Supreme Court of India hold a secret.

If this work comes out today, all Public-Sector Undertakings (PSUs) would be split tomorrow and handed over to the states. Why should a chief justice hailing from Assam conceal this work from the eye of the people? Is this work not a fact? The secrecy of this work gives the impression that the present Chief Justice of India asked the media to keep the happenings in the Supreme Court of India a tight secret. Otherwise, at least one newspaper or TV channel might have informed the salient points of this work to the people.

Everything is in the hand of the Chief Justice of India. The people expect **an intelligent** answer from him tomorrow or day after tomorrow.

# 9

# A financial enterprise

The Congress Party, immediately after the interview of former judge of the Supreme Court of India *Kurian Joseph*, on 3 December 2018, demanded an independent judicial probe into the issues arising out of his remarks about the former Chief Justice of India, Dipak Misra. But the party failed to notice that the same charges were applicable to the present Chief Justice of India also.

Everyone wants to control the Chief Justice of India. The Government of India wants to control him when he tends to do justice. The people want to control him when he tends to do injustice.

**To the chief Justice of India, it is all a question of running a financial enterprise. A financial enterprise demands:** 1.He must annul the effects of the Directive Principles of the Constitution of India. 2. He must deny the benefits of Article 19 of the Constitution to the people and 3. He should not hesitate to invade the assets of the people.

Now the Chief Justice of India has no more to fear than the present man's work. Therefore, he denies freedom to Indians.

# 10

# Promoting by destruction

The CBI Joint Director, *Mr. A.K. Sharma*, on 4 December 2018, submitted before the Delhi High Court that the CBI Special Director, *Mr. Asthana*, was running an extortion racket in the CBI. He added that *Mr. Asthana* was the kingpin of all cognizable offences. He cited the complaint of *Mr. Sathish Sana Babu* – a Hyderabad businessman-, intercepted phone conversations and WhatsUp messages.

The Prime Minister of India, *Mr. Narendra Modi,* on 4 December 2018, said that the previous UPA Government alienated the public resources through third parties or so-called 'benamies'. The implied meaning of his revelation is that the Supreme Court of India had connived at the alienation of the public resources by the UPA Government.

The UPA Government approved the alienation of 34 Public Sector Undertakings (PSUs) by the predecessor NDA Government.

It alienated the HZL, Mumbai Airport and the Delhi Airport. The HZL alone yields a profit of over Re.50000 crore per year.

It alienated the coal, spectrum, iron ore and other natural resources to its promoters.

It sent the Pension Fund and the Provident Fund to unknown destinations.

When this man informed the illegal plundering citing different sections of the Constitution of India as and when they happened, the Supreme Court of India, Central Bureau of Investigation (CBI), Chief Vigilance Commissioner (CVC), the National Human Rights Commission (NHRC), Prime Minister of India,  President of India, High Courts, Newspapers, TV channels and the blogs concealed them from the eye of the people under the pretexts such as 'Freedom has limitations, 'One cannot level unfounded allegations', 'One should not damage the image of the institutions and individuals', 'There is no truth in it, 'Our TV channel is not for his growth' 'What can we do if the media don't publish his view', 'We cannot carry others on our shoulders'.

In fact, one cannot expect the media to inform this work to the people because they cannot be charitable to the extent of losing their ownership.

The Supreme Court of India also cannot enforce freedom of expression without divesting them of their ownership.

This condition enables the Prime Minister of India to proclaims to the world that the UPA Government committed illegalities. The opposition parties also find it easy to level such charges against him. The Supreme Court of India finds nothing wrong it.

The media occasionally warn the Supreme Court of India.

Yet the Supreme Court of India digests such things in the pretext of freedom of speech

Thus, the court grants freedom to the ruling class and not to anyone representing the 1000 million absent class citizens

The Government of Delhi handed over to the Tata Trust. Re. 1000 crore in the pretext of clearing the electricity dues.

The present NDA Government alienated a huge amount of natural assets immediately after assuming power. Further, it handed over Re.59000 crore to the Reliance Industries Limited (RIL) and others through 1000 million third parties. If the Government had not granted this amount, the RIL would not have extracted this money from the public. It is a corrupt method to transmit public money into the private pockets. The Chief Justice of India does not want the people to know this trick. In this way, he commits acts of corruption.

Tata Trust is a charitable trust. A Trustee cannot be a beneficiary of a charitable trust. Yet, the Supreme Court of India allowed the conversion of Tata Trust into a public limited company.

Therefore, 655 letters submitted to the Chief Justice of India remain concealed.

After the letter No. 645, the present man submitted 9 letters to the present Chief Justice of India. These letters are not sent to the media, blogs, President of India or any others because no one is ready to inform them to the people.

Therefore, the Chief Justice of India alone knows the contents of the last 9 letters.

The Prime Minister's Office might have asked the present Chief Justice - at least nine times - not to release these letters to the media. 'Don't let the people know our secret. Let them guess anything. If you let the people know it, they would make him the Prime Minister of India'. This is the only demand of the PMO. Therefore, the Chief Justice keeps this work as a secret one.

If he is a man acting in good faith, he would release those letters. Otherwise, he would find a pretext to conceal them.

The Union Government, on 5 December 2018, told the Supreme Court of India that *CBI Director Mr. Alok Varma* was sent on leave not because of any corruption charges against him but because he and *Joint Director Mr. Asthana* had been fighting like Kilkenny cats. The court wasted it's time for one more day and reserved the judgement on 6 December 2018.

If he received any money from anyone, he would be put to death.

If he did not receive any bribe from anyone, he would be reinstated.

The judges in the bench are not likely to **promote themselves by the destruction of the court** by taking a middle path.

# 11

# Our masters

A Public Interest Litigation (PIL) filed by a lawyer, on 6 December 2018, demanded a probe into the allegation of retired *Supreme Court of India judge Kurian Joseph* that the previous Chief Justice of India, *Mr. Dipak Misra,* was 'remote controlled' and that he was working under 'external influences'. The PIL sought an urgent hearing to maintain the credibility of the institution.

The Chief Justice of India replied that the credibility of the court is not affected by newspaper reports but by the people at the helm or by people who man it.

The Chief Justice of India is remote controlled not only by the people but also by the Prime Minister of India. What is important is whether the Chief Justice of India is constitutional in ways or not.

The message of what *Justice Kurian Joseph* said is that the then Chief Justice of India was remote controlled to perpetrate an illegitimate rule in India by denying freedom of expression.

Declining an urgent hearing to the PIL, the Chief Justice said that he would do his duty. He added that everyone must do his duty.

Curiously, the media did not reveal the identity of the advocate in the PIL. The media has stopped reporting the views of former Union Ministers *Mr. Arun Shourie* and *Mr. Yashwant Sinha.* It gives the impression that someone intercepts the emails of the present man or the present Chief Justice of India shared the contents of the letters he received from the present man with someone outside the court.

The Chief Justice of India need not share the contents of the letters from this writer with anyone, if he cannot inform the salient features of the 645 letters received by his predecessors to the people all over India. This is to pre-empt the media and the political leaders from taking counter measures.

The political leaders in India did violence specifically against Article 19 and the Article 39 of the Constitution of India. Some float as leaders by changing sides. So, some of them are union ministers for more than four decades. The media project them as political leaders because they are the beneficiaries of their action. For this, they keep the people like the present man away from the system and constantly discuss not ideas but individuals and events.

Some political leaders maintain TV channels using their ill-gotten wealth. Some do not possess anything but are the slaves of the former.

If the award of the common man is enforced, the people would come to know men and matters according to degree and a new breed of political leaders would appear to run the nation. The present political leaders would become as obscure as the present man now.

The Supreme Court of India can reject this suggestion and take any other action to enforce freedom of expression although it is bound to fail.

At the instance of the Chief Justice of India, the Prime Minister of India, *Mr. Narendra Modi*, paid a visit to the Court No.1 of the Supreme Court of India, and shared the table with the Chief Justice of India for a dinner he hosted for the judges of the BIMSTEC (Bay of Bengal Initiative for Multi Sectoral Technical and Economic Co-operation) countries (Bangladesh, India, Bhutan, Nepal, Myanmar and Thailand) on November 25, 2018. No other prime minister had done this since the inauguration of the court by the then Prime Minister of India, *Mr. Jawaharlal Nehru,* 60 years ago.

The media reported the above only on 6 December 2018 after studying its pros and cons. At last, the media might have felt that it would be a boon for his 2019 election.

Prime Minister of India did not face a free and fair election to seize power.

He did not restore the illegally privatized Public-Sector Undertakings (PSUs) or the money in the Pension Fund and the Provident Fund.

He alienated the natural resources in the pretext of auction. He did this by doing violence to the Article 39 of the Constitution of India.

One half of the people cannot afford to buy gas. This section, needs gas subsidy.  Instead, the Prime Minister of India gives gas subsidy to the existing gas consumers. This is to hike the price for the benefit of his promoters at will. Thus, he, illegally gave Re,59000 crore to his promoters and others. It is an act of corruption copied from the Chief Minister of Delhi.

He received 645 letters through the President of India. Yet he did not inform it to the people. Thus, he did violence against Article 19 and kept the people like animals.

Therefore, the present Prime Minister of India forfeited his right to sit beside the Chief Justice of India.

If a Prime of India does his duty, he deserves the respect of the people and the Chief Justice of India.

In contrast, if he commits one illegality after another in bad faith, the Chief Justice of India cannot see eye to eye with him. In such a situation, the Chief Justice of India must consult all judges and give his final award before sitting beside him. Alternatively, he should have informed the salient features of the 655 letters before inviting him. Then, one would think that the Chief Justice did his duty to the nation without fear or favor.

Now, the Chief Justice of India makes the people believe that the Prime Minister of India is doing his work wonderfully.


Recently retired *Supreme Court of India judge Kurian Joseph* on 6 December 2018 said, ***"We are public servants. We are serving the public. The public are our masters. Do the people see that we are serving them?"***

He explains why the judges must obey the people as and when they demand freedom. Apparently, he had been influenced by the present man. Even a silent judge like *Kurian Joseph* finds it difficult to abstract himself from more than 645 letters!

What factors limited his work in the Supreme Court of India? Nothing is known. If he continues like this, the system would strange his views.

# 12

# A crime

*CBI Director Mr. Alok Varma,* on 7 December 2018, told the Delhi High Court, that there were very serious incriminating evidences to prove that *Special CBI Director Mr. Asthana* had been running an extortion racket using his office. As the Government had divested *Mr. Alok Varma* of his duties, the court asked him to submit an affidavit in a sealed cover through the CBI.

All Chief Justices of India since June 2001 have been promoting an extortion racket in India. For this, they deny freedom to the people. The direct consequence is the formation of illegitimate governments. The present Chief Justice of India can give freedom to the people to stop it.

*Prime Minister of India Mr. Narendra Modi,* on 7 December 2018, said that the economic offenders would be brought to justice even if they escape from India.

He is the No.1 economic offender in India. The gas subsidy scheme is an example for it. The people should not know this. So, he did not inform the 645 letters submitted to the President of India to the people. Thus, he simply denies freedom. It is a cognizable offence.

The Supreme Court of India cannot connive at the above. Yet it happens. Therefore, the Chief Justice of India has been running an extortion racket in India.

If the present Chief Justice of India is a lover of freedom, he can prevent it after informing this work to the people.

An advocate, *Mr. ML. Sharma,* on 7 December 2018, filed a Public Interest Litigation (PIL) in the Supreme Court of India accusing *Finance Minister of India Mr. Arun Jaitely* of plundering the capital reserve of the Reserve Bank of India (RBI).

The infuriated bench headed by *Chief Justice of India Ranjan Gogoi* dismissed it and imposed a fine of Re.50,000 on him.

The bench said that the petitioner should not have made *Finance Minister Mr. Arun Jaitely* the main party in the PIL. The meaning of the petition as interpreted by bench was that *Mr. Arun Jaitely* (and not the Government) wanted to plunder the capital reserves of the RBI.

Apparently, the 2G spectrum case was based on a PIL filed by this advocate. He could succeed in cancelling hundreds of licenses that were granted by the UPA Government based on the first-come-first serve policy. The ridiculous aspect of the case was that the court approved the licenses granted by the NDA Government under the same policy. The people felt that the manipulators had a hand in the judgement and on the advocate. They deplored the silence of other judges of the Supreme Court of India in this matter. Some other PILs filed by him were similarly related.

In this matter, the court could have asked him to file an affidavit to know the meaning of the word 'plundering' mentioned by him. Now, the decree has the effect of glorifying *Mr. Arun Jaitely.*

*Mr. Arun Jaitely* does not deserve a position in the Union Cabinet because he is not a product of democracy. In an atmosphere of freedom, he might not have become a political leader at all. All other political leaders in India are similarly related.

It must be noted that the present man had demanded the Supreme Court of India, many times, to hand over the surplus money extracted by the RBI for imports to the Government. As the court did not let the people to know this, it is suspected that the RBI siphons off the foreign exchange to unknown destinations.

*Mr. Arun Jaitely* had been a powerful minister under *Prime Minister Mr. A. B. Vajpayee.* He helped privatize 34 Public Sector Undertakings (PSUs) at that time even without enacting a law for that purpose. The Constitution of India does not allow it. Parliament did not allow it. Under these conditions, even the guidelines devised for privatization were violated! Thus, he openly did violence to Article 39 of the Constitution of India. As a constitutional lawyer, he should have told the Cabinet that Article 39 together with Article 19 forms the essence of the Constitution of India. He did not do so.

Anyone doing anything in conflict with Article19 and 39 must remain in jail because the judges send even small offenders to jail for doing something in conflict with the Constitution of India. But the judges harbor them in the court and use complimentary words and gestures forgetting their anti-constitutional acts. Moreover, the judges shield them from public criticism. Therefore, they rule India.

This happened because the Supreme Court of India wanted to do a premeditated injustice in 2001.

Excepting for the accident of birth in India, the people have no connection with the Supreme Court of India. Yet, the present man dared to point out the Constitution of India to it. In a minute, the innocent head of the Constitution of India rolled in the dust as the court described it as a policy decision. The present man kept sending more and more letters to the then President of India, *Mr. K. R. Narayanan.* He went to the Supreme Court of India with the letter in vain. The judges asked him not to interfere in their work. He said that the common man would save India.

*President of India Dr. A.P.J. Abdul Kalam* applied brake to the privatization programme. But he could not give freedom.

In the meantime, the Central Bureau of Investigation (CBI) refused to accept letters. Therefore, the present man stopped sending letters to the CBI, Central Vigilance Commissioner (CVC) and the National Human Rights Commission (NHRC),

The letters were sent to the newspapers and the, TV channels all over the world. The letters were sent to the world leaders and the UN and this strained the relationship with some countries. But none of letters were able to enlighten the enraged Chief Justice of India or his successors. Soon the Supreme Court of India was filled with corpses. The air reeked with the sickening stench of partly buried letters from the present man. Some judges began to look with apprehension at the cold-blooded act of the court. *Justices S. Rajendra Babu* and *G.P. Mathur,* on 16 September 2003, gave expression to their disapproval through the HPCL-BPCL judgement.

Just at that moment some parties dragged in with difficulty the strange looking Constitution that was struggling for its worth. The present man again pointed out the threatened loss of liberty. Being in a slightly chastened mood, *Chief Justice K.G. Balakrishnan* from the Kerala State and *Justice Sathasivam* from the Tamil Nadu State discarded the loyalty concept with great difficulty and a three-judge bench headed by *Chief Justice K.G. Balakrishnan,* on 7 May 2010, declared that the natural resources must remain with the Government.

After that, a wave of pity swept through the cruel heart of the Supreme Court of India, but the judgement did not penetrate its intellect as the people lost all hope of getting an intelligent answer from it.

*President of India Mrs. Pratibha Devisingh Patel,* restrained the banks from buying shares. The manipulators had to borrow money from the banks. She started returning the action taken report to a few letters. Maharastra Police raided her house in retaliation. She said that she chose not to cut down the tree to pluck some fruits.

Her successor, *Mr.Pranab Mukherjee,* managed everything with the so-called Pranab effects. Therefore, the present man stopped sending letters to him.

When *Mr. Ram Nath Kovind* became the President of India, the present man sent a letter to save *Justice Karnan.* But he could not. Another letter was sent in vain to save the life *Miss. Anitha* from the NEET episode. All newspapers and all TV channels all over the world were again contacted for the freedom of Indians. Simultaneously, a series of high intensity letters were sent to him to enlighten the constitutional points. He was amazed to go through the letters because none in India ever mentioned such points. However, the system annulled all his actions by sharing and by maintaining great secrecy. He could not give freedom.

Now, the letters are being sent to the present Chief Justice of India only and he is being asked not to share the contents with anyone outside the court before publishing the earlier letters. This is purely for political reasons.

The chief justices of the Supreme Court of India committed a mistake because they allowed a policy that conflicted with the essence of the Constitution of India. The mistake became a cognizable offence when they failed to inform the letters to the public. They did not enforce their May 7, 2010 judgement also.

These were later given in the books- *Prime Minister Mr. A.B. Vajpayee and the Abdication of Power, The Warring among Dr.A.P.J. Adul Kalam, Dr. Manmohan Singh and Mrs. Sonia Gandhi, A Madonna of India Vol 1 and 2. The Pranab Effects Vol 1 and We Will Strange You - India Under Prime Minister Mr. Narendra Modi Vol 1.*

The media must maintain an informed citizenry. It is the duty of the newspapers and the TV channels to inform everything that happened to the people because of the letters. Then only the people would know what is right and what is wrong. But they concealed everything from them. They could very easily subvert the Constitution of India. They simply undermined democracy in India. The total loss suffered by the present man and the 1000 million absent class citizens cannot be calculated.

Therefore, all registered newspapers and the TV channels in India must be confiscated and their owners sent to jail before informing the salient features of the 657 letters to the people. For this, the Chief Justice of India must constitute an appropriate bench to issue the necessary orders. It is his duty. This would **give life to the nation.**

The recently retired judges of the Supreme Court of India, *Justice Kurian Joseph*, on 7 December 2018, said, ***"If a man does not do what is right, it is a crime."***

His every word seems to lurk some inner meaning. Everyone says that one must fight against illegality and injustice. Everyone says that one must do his duty. But *Justice Kurian Joseph* says that when someone thinks that something is right, he must do that. 'If I do this, others would say this and that. So, I am not going to do a different thing for my reputation'. He says that the act of taking such a stand is a crime.

What prompted him to talk like this?

He had been sitting with the present Chief Justice of India in the important PIL bench till his retirement. From where he said the above is not important but what he said is important. Does he say this to the present Chief Justice of India?

# 13

# The illiterate people

Speaking at the Second Dadachanji Memorial debate, a sitting judge of the Supreme Court of India, Justice *Madan B. Lokur,* said, *"I think we are comparatively far more restrained than other jurisdictions".*

No apex court anywhere in the world might have concealed from the discerning eye of the people 657 letters out of fear or loyalty. But the Supreme Court of India and the President of India directly or indirectly shared them with the media but not the people. This is treachery.

The letters emitted a foul vapor, sickening to the senses of the judges. *Justice Lokur* considered the act of concealing the letters as a crime against humanity. Therefore, he said that the judges are more restrained than their peers in other countries.

Then the Attorney General of India, *Mr. K.K. Venugopal,* retorted that the Supreme Court of India "garnered to itself vast powers which no one apex court in the world has ever exercised and its interpretation of the

Article 142 conveyed that it was above the law. He explained the meaning of 'complete justice' and rejected the concept "constitutional morality.

Then, he put the illiteracy of Indians at 26 percent. He added that *"even **the illiterate people** know what is good for them. And therefore, for the court to believe unless we interfere, the country is doomed, I say no, it can't"*.

The Attorney General did not demand the judges to take a middle path in the *Alok Varma case*. But he certainly demanded that they should not tell the illiterate people in India the outstanding features of the 657 letters.

Therefore, if the Chief Justice of India thinks that the act of telling the people this is a right thing to do, he must do it today and not tomorrow.

Then, *Mr. Venugopal* would see a democratically elected - legitimate - Government in India for the first time.

# 14

# Losing the honour and majesty?

The leaders of the 21 opposition political parties in India, on 10 December 2018, gathered at Delhi and alleged that the *Mr. Narendra Modi-led* NDA Government subverted the Constitution of India and made democracy a mockery. They resolved to defeat it in the 2019 General Election to save the Constitution of India, to protect democracy and to preserve freedom.

The above political parties played a complementary role to the *Mr. A.B. Vajpayee- led* NDA Government. When they seized power, they chose not to restore the illegally privatized Public-Sector Undertakings (PSUs) or the natural resources. They simply repeated the alienation of national assets by doing violence to Articles 39 and 19 of the Constitution of India.

They exist as political leaders only because of their above actions. During this process, they augmented their illegal wealth. Now they have strong financial clout. Many own TV stations to air their views.

As the Supreme Court of India support the denial of freedom, the people are being constrained to support them.

When the Election results of five States were trickling in, the Government of India selected former Finance Secretary to the Government of India, *Mr. Shaktikanta Das* as the Governor of the Reserve Bank of India (RBI). It appears as the second good faith action of Prime Minister of India *Mr. Narendra Modi*, the first being the selection of *Mr. Ram Nath Kovind* for the post of the President of India.

The Congress Party-led opposition parties defeated the BJP -led ruling parties in the elections to Rajasthan, Chhattisgarh and Madya Pradesh States and in Telangana and Meghalaya States, the reginal parties defeated them.

*Chief Justice of India Ranjan Gogoi* rigged the elections. The rigging is more heinous than those rigged by his predecessor, *Justice Dipak Misra,* because the former had come out of the Supreme Court of India for the freedom of Indians.

During the farewell function to *Justice Kurian Joseph, Chief Justice of India Ranjan Gogoi* said that **the judges were losing the honor and majesty of office.**

A man of honor is always a lover of truth. Did he tell anything about the 658 letters received by the Chief Justices of India since June 1, 2001 or the 13 letters he received after assuming charge as the Chief Justice of India?

The Chief Justice of India must do what is right to protect freedom, democracy and the rule of the Constitution.

"If I do what is right as per the Constitution, others would say that I am doing this for adding to my reputation or in private interest. So, I don't want to do this.' The people do not expect such an answer from the Chief Justice of India.

Why did the present man not place such a demand so far to any other Chief Justice of India?

There exists a significant difference between the possession of power and the occasion for its exercise. The present man approaches the present Chief Justice of India only after exhausting all other options – the present President of India included. However, there exists a feeling that the President of India would stand by the Chief Justice of India to establish freedom to Indians.

# 15

# A talented man?

Editor-in- Chief of a Tamil TV channel, *Thanthi TV, Mr. Rangaraja Pandey,* on 11 December 2018, resigned from his lucrative post. The *Thanthi TV* had been a subscriber to the YouTube channel of the present man. Apparently, he was not allowed to report the views of the present man. Some of his questions reflected the things present in the blogs. Now, even if he makes public his grievances, the media might not report them.

The media, on 11 December 2018, said that election results to five states showed the ability of *Mr. Rahul Gandhi* to take on the BJP.

It is not the ability of *Mr. Rahul Gandhi* but the ability of the Chief Justice of India to deny freedom to Indians. He simply rigs the elections.

The reluctance of the Prime Minister of India, *Mr. Narendra Modi*, to give freedom to Indians even after the defeat shows that he prefers a dynasty represented by *Mr. Rahul Gandhi* rather than a common man.

The Supreme Court of India, on 11 December 2018, reiterated its decision to impose a fine of Re.50000 on an advocate for dragging the name of Union Minister *Mr. Arun Jaitely*, through a frivolous Public Interest Litigation (PIL).

A bench headed by Chief Justice of India *Ranjan Gogoi* heard the revision petition.

The Chief Justice of India got time to know the problem of advocate *Mr. ML. Sharma.* But he did not get any time to tell the illiterate population of India the contents of 659 letters addressed to the Chief Justice of India or the action taken by his predecessors on them.

In the farewell function of *Justice Kurian Joseph,* he said that he was finding it difficult to identify suitable replacements in his court as the talented people refuse to become judges. The message was that **he is a talented man** for adjudicating cases.

Assume that Chief Justice of India *Rangan Gogoi* is **a man of many talents.** Then his talents must be serviceable to the nation.

But he utilizes his talents to conceal hundreds of letters from the public.

The people are entitled to know the functioning of the judiciary. But, he is not ready to respond.

The Union Government, on 11 December 2018, invited tenders to sell its Air India building at Mumbai for about Re.2000 crore. The sale, before enforcing freedom of expression, is an unconstitutional act.

In this matter, Chief Justice of India acts in bad faith.

There are courts in some countries to control the judges if they act in bad faith. In India, the impeachment is the only remedy and it is not easy.

# 16

# The Tata Trust

The National Company Law Appellate Tribunal (NCLAT) today resumed its hearing over the batch of petitions filed by ousted Chairman of the Tata Group, Mr. Cyrus Mistry, and the two investment firms supporting him.

It gives the impression that the present Chief Justice of India – in bad faith - gave his tacit permission to resume the hearing.

**The Tata Trust is a charitable trust.** The trustees of a charitable trust cannot be its beneficiaries. The tussle between *Mr. Tata* and *Mr. Mistry* gives the impression that they committed a cognizable offence by being its beneficiaries.

Further, the Tata Trust passed a resolution to convert it into a limited company. The charitable trusts are irrevocable trusts. They are forbidden from passing such resolutions. The Chief Justice of India did not allow the law to take its course by denying freedom of expression.

Furthermore, the Tata Trust enjoyed the benefits of a charitable trust from the Government. Yet, the Government remains as a silent spectator.

The Chief Justice of India alone knows whether the registration authority of a charitable trust and a company is one and the same or not. If different, the Tata Trust would not come under the jurisdiction of the NCLAT. It would come under the registrar of trusts or any other competent authority.

These things were pointed out to the predecessors of the present Chief Justice of India. They did not tell it to the illiterate people of India but hid everything in a corner of the Supreme Court of India. 'It is always nice to know that every chief justice of India is doing this, although they would not go any further than that'.

The media, on 11 December 2018, reported that the Government of India would meet its disinvestment target in this fiscal year. The media, further, said that 53 per cent shares of the Rural Electrification Corporation (REC) have been sold.

The above sales do violence to Articles 19 and 39.

Did the people of Assam or the North-East get any share in the REC. Alas, they get bullets intermittently?

The present man earlier said this in the letter No.41 dated 10-10-2004.

The then President of India, *Dr. A.P.J. Abdul Kalam* and the then Chief Justice of India restrained the Government from selling the shares. The Government is doing this unconstitutional act without much publicity now.

The Chief Justice of India should not cover up the unconstitutional deeds of the Government of India. He should tell **the illiterate people** the salient features of the letters he received from the people.

Where will the employment opportunities go after privatization? Does it not violate Article 16 of the Constitution of India?

Why should a chief justice hailing from Assam permit it that too after offending Article 19 of the Constitution of India?

Does he remember the salt he ate?

There is no hidden ambiguity in the Constitution of India. The Chief Justice of India must read Articles 16, 19 and 39 in the light of the entire Constitution of India and give his reply to the present man, if not to the people at large.

# 17

# A darker period?

The Congress Party, on 14 December 2018, selected *Mr. Kamal Nath,* for the post of the Chief Minister of Madhya Pradesh State.

Just as Union Minister *Mr. Arun Jaitely* is to the BJP Party, *Mr. Kamal Nath* is to the Congress Party.

It is pertinent to recall that sharing a dais with Union Commerce Minister *Mr. Kamal Nath*, on 25 October 2004, *Mr. Arun Jaitely* -in an obvious reference to the present man- said, "Even if one blinks then nothing moves".

In his reply, *Mr. Kamal Nath* said, "There was no compromise on the route started in 1991. The UPA Government is committed to privatization"

Thus, the ruling class does not distinguish between *Mr. Arun Jaitely* and *Mr. Kamal Nath.*

The selection of *Mr.Kamal Nath* shows that the ruling class would determine the chief ministers also so long as *Mr. Rahul Gandhi* and *Mr. Narendra Modi* are at the helm of their parties. Therefore, what the people see is not the will of the people but the manifestation of the will of the ruling class.

The other chief ministers are similarly related.

These are the consequences of the rigged elections.


A bench of the Supreme Court of India comprising *Chief Justice of India Ranjan Gogoi, Justice S.K. Kaul* and *Justice K.M. Joseph,* on14 December 2018, approved the Re.59000 crore *Rafale* fighter jet deal.

It said that the Government had followed the due process before finalizing the deal.

The Prime Minister of India did not seek the approval of the Union Cabinet before finalizing the deal. Therefore, the court – in very bad faith- told a lie to deceive the people.

In a Cabinet System of Government, a prime minister must obtain the approval of his Cabinet. To this extent, that deal is unconstitutional.

The court or the petitioners did not want to know the reason why the Government did not seek better jets from the USA or the reason for not inviting an international tender.

After the judgement, a petitioner advocate. *Mr. Prasant Bhusan,* said that the bench added certain things that were not on record. The inference was that the bench liaised with the Government secretly to write the judgement. This proves that a conspiracy exists behind every judgement involving public money.

But no petitioners pointed out Articles 14, 16, 19 or 39 to enlighten the court during the hearing. Thus, the petitioners scored a same side goal.

The court justified the *offset clause* saying that it lacked the necessary expertise to judge it.

Whenever the court does something unconstitutional, it strikes ignorance. This time, it tells that it lacks necessary expertise.

The court should not tell this as a reason for the its judgement because it accepts that it is incompetent to adjudicate the case. In such a condition, the Chief Justice of India should not have taken keen interest to hear the case. He should have constituted another bench with competent judges.

**The judgement of the Supreme Court of India must be definite, certain and as concise as possible. The judgement must contain the opinion stating the valid reasons for the decision.**

For instance, it says, that the adversaries possess 4th and 5th generation aircraft. But the Government opted for the 3rd generation aircraft. How can the court justify it when there were far better aircraft?

However, the crucial point is whether the deal is a constitutional one or not. To determine this, the judges must know the meaning of important Articles and the significance of the language used.

The deal provides for an offset clause. This clause allows the Government to transmit public money into the hand of its promoters through a third party. This subverts Articles 14 and 39 of the Constitution of India. To materialize this deal, the Government and the Supreme Court of India must deny freedom of expression. Therefore, this vitiates Article 19.

As for as possible, the court should not invoke any other Article or sentence or phrase in the Constitution and give a meaning other than that expressed in the above Articles. It should take the Constitution as a whole.

The deal is, therefore, trebly unconstitutional. In fact, it is terribly unconstitutional because it is against the essence of the Constitution of India.

As there is a substantial question of law, the court must refer this matter to a constitutional bench comprising judges capable interpreting the Constitution of India. Alternatively, the court must disclose the contents of the letters to the illiterate people of India.

If the Chief Justice of India is not ready for both, the nation is heading for a darker period and a series of **unconstitutional and antisocial judgements** could be expected under him.

# 18

# Add to the knowledge of the people

The Reserve Bank of India (RBI) Central Board that met under its new Governor, *Mr. Shaktikanta Das,* discussed currency management and financial literacy. The media reported it on, on 15 December 2018.

What does it mean by financial literacy? Apparently, the Governor discussed the idea of the present man to take the surplus money extracted for imports for public welfare.

The media on 15 December 2018, said that BJP lost Madhya Pradesh despite getting more votes. The crowd support showed that the BJP lagged the Congress Party. But the seats tallied with the exit poll prediction. So, this poll might be a rehearsal for manipulating the Electronic Voting Machine (EVM) in the 2019 General Election to the Parliament. **Therefore, voting must be by ballot. This is a fundamental right of the people.** The Government of India, the Supreme Court of

India, the Election Commission of India and the ruling class shall not join to take away this right.

*Mr. Rahul Gandhi,* Congress Party President and leader of the Opposition in the Parliament, said that *Prime Minister of India Mr.Modi* was a thief and *Mr. Anil Ambani* a beneficiary of the *Rafale deal.* The media reported it on 15 December 2018. He vowed to prove it.

To give a clean chit to the *Rafale agreement,* the Supreme Court of India – in its judgement- pointed out that the Comptroller and Auditor General (CAG) audited the offset clause of the *Rafale deal* and the Public Account Committee (PAC) examined the CAG report. The court said that it did not possess the necessary expertise to judge them but inferred that due process was followed and gave a verdict in favor of the deal.

The advocate for the petitioner, *Mr. Prasant Bhusan,* told the people that the statement of the court was a lie.

A petitioner, *Mr.Arun Shourie,* said that a man contacted the judges of the bench and misled them. He wanted the court to disclose the identity of that man. He added that the court granted license to the government to do wrong things and the court was on trial for an unethical conspiracy.

*Mr. Arun Shourie* sold 34 Public Sector Undertaking (PSUs) by doing violence against Article 39 and 19.  He had welcomed the BALCO judgement although court had granted license to do all sorts of wrong things. As there is no freedom, he has become a crusader against corruption.

The Government disowned the judgement and wanted the court to make a correction in the judgement. It told the court that the Government did not obtain the CAG report although it is the normal procedure. The PAC also did not examine the CAG report. The government accordingly wanted a correction in the judgement. Thus, it drags the court to mud just as it dragged former French President.

According to the doctrine of judicial stability, once the judgement is pronounced, the court loses the power to amend, modify, alter or correct it. The judges are denied the power to add or modify or correct their own judgements.

The Government of India has the right to determine what aircraft is to be purchased, when it is to be purchased and how it is to be purchased.

As it is something connected with the security of the nation, the Government has an obligation to tell the court that it bought the best available item and the court, in turn, must look at the face of the people and tell them that the attempt made by the Government to buy a better one failed. But the court should not tell the people that the Government did not seek a better one.

In the present case, the implied meaning of the judgement is that the Government did not seek a better one and it is treasonable offence.

The offset clause of the *Rafale agreement* provides for the siphoning of the revenues of the Government of India to a few private individuals. Their only qualification is their ability to control the public thought.

The amount being siphoned off could be Re. thirty thousand crore, 3 lakh crore or 30 lakh crore. The amount would be given as and when the offset partners demand.

At the same time, the people are being sent to jail for Re.3, 30, 300 or 3000 by the Supreme Court of India for the slightest conflict with the Constitution of India. It even punished a conductor for about thirty tickets and a political leader for Re.42 lakh.

The Supreme Court of India is responsible for this condition.

The above offset policy conflicts with Article 39 of the Constitution of India. **In any conflict between an agreement and the written Constitution of a nation, the Constitution would prevail.**

What the present man says is different from what all others in India say. In fact, the people, the advocates and the judges have no knowledge about the legal and constitutional points mentioned by the present man. These points are not to educate the Chief Justice of India but to **add to the knowledge of the people**.

If the illiterate people get a chance to hear about these letters, the people would get reasonable judgements. Now there is nothing but darkness ahead, but the Chief Justice can turn on the light at any time.

# 19

# 'A reasonable man standard'

The Union Cabinet, on 17 December 2018, decided to increase the LPG penetration in India to 100 per cent. It is a panic reaction to the last few letters

Despite the above decision, the Prime Minister of India, *Mr. Narendra Modi,* would continue to be the No.1 economic offender in India. The reasons were given earlier.

Former Union Minister for Disinvestments *Mr. Arun Shourie,* on 16 December 2018, said that the *Rafale judgement* showed the perils of "sealed cover'. As the Supreme Court of India sought the details of the *Rafale deal in* sealed covers, he talked like this.

The present man repeatedly said that the Supreme Court of India should not ask the parties to give anything in sealed covers. The people did not hear it.

But, when *Mr. Arun Shourie* said the same thing, the people hear it.

What is the difference between the two persons?

*Mr. Arun Shourie* is an author, journalist, economist and politician. He worked as an editor of newspapers. He has been doing everything for the enslavement of Indians for the last 18 years. As a union minister, he helped privatize 34 Public Sector Undertakings (PSUs) by doing violence to Article 39 and 19. Many people remain in jail for far smaller offences.

The present man is an author, economist, historian and politician. He worked as a lecturer. He has been working for the freedom of Indians for the last 18 years. The present man saved many PSUs from privatization.

*Mr. Shourie* worked as an editor. He has written many books. Besides, he opposes the *Rafale agreement* long after the present man mentioned it to the Chief Justice of India.

The present man has written 15 books, sent 663 letters to the Chief Justice of India for freedom and given hundreds of concrete suggestions for the welfare of 1000 million people. Besides he has propounded 'The Predicate Theory' for English language teaching.

Whether the people must hear *Mr. Arun Shourie* or the present man?

The Chief Justice of India must give an answer.


The Government of India, on 17 December 2018, moved the Supreme Court of India seeking a correction in the *Rafale judgement*. The petition proves that the bench wrote the judgement based on the wrong statements given by the Government in the sealed covers. Alternatively, the insatiable desire of the bench to justify bad faith actions led to a wrong judgement.

**The bench now knows that it has no appellate jurisdiction or power of review. It cannot correct its judgement.**

The judges of the Supreme Court must have full knowledge about various Articles of the Constitution of India. They must take the meaning of the instrument.

No man can be an expert in every field. It is the limitation of nature. However, if a judge thinks that he is not 'competent' to judge a case, he should not hear it. Similarly, if a Chief Justice of India thinks that he lacks the necessary 'expertise' to adjudicate a case, he should hand over it to other judges.

If a judge 'fills up' a constitution or law or policy with incompetency or lack of expertise, that judgement is null and void. Therefore, the *Rafale judgement* is not a valid one.

The crucial point is that the judges must act in good faith while adjudicating the cases. They must apply **'a reasonable man standard'** to take the decision.

When a judge uses 'a reasonable man standard' the question of incompetency or lack of expertise simply disappears.

If a judge acts in bad faith, the instrument becomes useless. The people begin to think that his judgements are not reasonable. They think that he has an axe to grind. Therefore, at no time, should the people think that the judgements are not reasonable.

When the judgements are not reasonable, the confidence of the public is shaken. Under such conditions the Chief Justice of India would not pick up courage to tell the illiterate people the nature of the letters he receives from the public.

*Justice Kurian Joseph,* after working very closely with the present Chief Justice of India says that the people have a right to know the working of the Supreme Court of India, and that the institution must respond to their concerns.

The Chief Justice of India need not obey *Justice Kurian Joseph* or the present man, but he must **obey law**. If the law demands that the illiterate people of India must know the contents of this letter, he must release it to the media.

# 20

# Knowing enough

The Government of India moved the Supreme Court of India, on 15 December 2018, for the correction of the *Rafale judgement*. But there are no reports about the action taken by the court for the last three days.

Once a bench of the Supreme Court of India pronounces a judgement, it has no further authority to amend, alter, change or otherwise add to or delete from the judgement. *It is also called the doctrine of 'res judicata'.*

As the advocates are not aware of this elementary principle in law, they moved the court. By strange luck, the Chief Justice of India got the benefit of the last two letters from the present man. But for them, the court might have made a day of it.

In fact, the Chief Justice of India has been striking terror into the hearts of the Government of India through the *Alok Varma case* and the *Rafale case.* Now everyone knows that the judgement was obtained without procedure required by law. It was un-supported by substantial evidence.

A judge of the Supreme Court of India need not be an erudite person in law, But he should be satisfied **that he knows 'enough'** to be able to decide a case.

Whatever happened, the views of the present man must be known to the people at least now.

The political leaders in India did violence against Article 39 and Article 19 directly or indirectly. They – the present Prime Minister of India included - must be in jail. The tragedy is that they alone are being heard in India. This is unconstitutional.

The present man represents the absent class citizens. He must be heard throughout the length breadth of India for the service he rendered to the nation in the last 18 years. No other man with lesser contribution to nation building should get greater coverage than the present man. This is for the freedom of the people. This is the constitutional right of the people.

If the Chief Justice of Indian thinks that some others deserve greater coverage, they must present their claims before him.

The present Chief Justice India must leave no stone unturned to achieve freedom to Indians. Then only the levers of power will be controlled by the real representatives of the people making the Government a legitimate one.

# 21

# Giving reverence to citizenry's rights

*Former Prime Minister of India, Dr.* Manmohan Singh, on 19 December 2018, said that he was not afraid of the media when he functioned as the Prime Minister of India. He said this to attack Prime Minister *Mr. Narendra Modi.*

The claim of *Dr. Manmohan Singh* is not a correct one because he answered only tutored questions of the media persons and not to the citizens of India.

Both refused to put right the public wrongs committed by their predecessors. Further, both did violence to the Article 19 with the purpose of doing violence against Article 39. To show fiscal deficit, both refused to take the real income of the Government although Prime Minister *Mr.Modi* takes some steps.

*Dr. Manmohan Singh* sent the money in the Provident Fund and the Pension Fund to unknown destinations. It went down as a heinous act.

If private individuals are involved in gas distribution, the gas price must depend on market conditions. But *Mr. Narendra Modi* transmitted a huge amount of money to his promoters through the gas subsidy policy. This and the offset policy cut the root of Article 39.

About the style of functioning, *Dr. Manmohan Singh* allowed his Cabinet Ministers to take decisions and carry them out without the approval of the Union Cabinet. In contrast, *Mr. Narendra Modi* took the decisions and carried them out without the approval of the Union Cabinet. Thus, both functioned in an unconstitutional way in private interest.

Former Chief Justice of India *Dipak Misra,* on 18 December 2018, said that the Supreme Court of India must ***give reverence for the citizenry's rights.***

In one sentence he has put everything – from the law of the shop to the Constitution. The citizens have a right to hear and to be heard. For this, the Supreme Court of India must have *reverence for the citizenry's rights*.

He had rigged the elections in bad faith. Now, he regrets that he did not give reverence for citizenry's rights during his stint in the Supreme Court of India.

There are no reports about the *Rafale judgement* correction moved before the *Rafale bench.*

**If a party proposes correction in the ambiguous language used by it in a court, the standard rule is to construe against the party.** Further, the Government would never get a favorable verdict even from a constitution bench because of two reasons:

Firstly, the Prime Minister of India did not place it in the Union Cabinet. A prime minister is forbidden from loading someone with riches under any pretext independently.

Secondly, the offset clause cuts the root of Article 39. The language of the Constitution of India does not leave Article 39 in doubt.

Therefore, the *Rafale agreement* is null and void. The demand of the petitioners was for a probe and not the cancellation of the agreement.

However, nothing is coming out of the Supreme Court of India. This gives the impression that it initiated action against the media houses for not reporting news and views according to degree. The media, in turn, might have decided to black out the orders of the Supreme Court of India. This is **a coup.**

Chief Justice of India must note that he projects the criminals as the leaders and conceals others relentlessly working for the well-being of the people.

He must interpret and apply the Constitution of India now.

# 22

# A free chief justice

The Vice President of India, **Mr. Venkaiah Naidu**, on 20 December 2018, said that there must be a code of conduct for the political leaders. The people all over India heard his views.

The political leaders known to the illiterate people of India did violence against Article 39 of the Constitution of India. For doing this, they did violence against Article 19. The illiterate people of India do not know this.

Therefore, all political leaders known to the illiterate people must be prosecuted. *Mr. Venkaiah Naidu* is one among them.

The Chief Justice of India should have restrained all newspapers and the TV channels under his jurisdiction from showing the above political leaders to the people. He should have, at least, asked the public-sector TV channels to refrain from showing them until a degree of importance list is prepared.

As the Prime Minister of India, *Mr. Narendra Modi,* and the Union Ministers did violence against Articles 39 and 19, they also should not be shown to the people. Their views and other political works also should not be reported. However, the Government is free to announce its policy decisions through the news readers.

As *Mr. Rahul Gandhi,* the leader of the opposition, induced the then Prime Minister of India, *Dr. Manmohan Singh,* to do violence against Articles 39 and 19, he might not appear in the degree of importance scale. As many other political leaders, directly or indirectly, did violence against Article 19, they also should not be shown to the people.

The above suggestion is to make *Chief Justice of India Ranjan Gogoi* a free chief justice. He shall not constitute any benches until he is free.

When the Chief Justice of India is free, he would agree that the enforcement of the Constitution of India - that impose affirmative duties on the media - is his duty. Until then, he might not agree that it is his duty.

Incidentally, this would go down as the first step to make the 2019 elections free and fair.

# 23

# Deception

Justice *Chelameswar*, a retired judge of the Supreme Court of India, on 20 December 2018, said, *"We tried to change the Supreme Court of India. But it has not improved even after Justice Ranjan Gogoi became the Chief Justice of India. The democratic institutions should not do injustice. But the Supreme Court of India is going wrong. The act of concealing it would not improve the situation. I might not have resorted to sealed cover procedure if I was hearing the Rafale case"*.

Justice *Chelameswar,* along with Justice *Ranjan Gogoi,* Justice *Kurian Joseph* and Justice *Madan B. Lokur* convened a press conference on 12 January 2018. Describing the press conference as an extra-ordinary one, the four judges said, "Certain issues afflicting the Supreme Court of India could destroy Indian democracy".

*Justice Chelameswar* has levelled a very serious allegation against Chief Justice of India *Ranjan Gogoi.* It is more serious than the one levelled against *Chief Justice Dipak Misra* by *Justice Ranjan Gogoi*. The Chief Justice should give an open reply to him.

*Mr.Prasant Bhusan*, an advocate for *Mr. Arun Shouie* and *Mr. Yaswant Sinha* in the *Rafale* case, on 20 December 2018, said that the judges relied on unsigned notes to write the judgement. He added that he would submit a petition for recalling the *Rafale* judgement.

The judges have some residual powers over their judgement. But, they cannot use this power for recalling their judgements or for correcting them. The advocates of the Supreme Court of India do not know this.

A larger bench can set aside the judgement. But *Chief Justice Ranjan Gogoi* has no moral right to constitute a larger bench for the *Rafale* case because the judgement would be a logical extension of his judgement only.

The advocates of the Supreme Court of India must investigate the constitutionality or otherwise of the agreements and policy decisions. But they very rarely do this.

The Prime Minister of India is not the Government of India, if he does not consider the Parliament or the Union Cabinet. He can bypass the Union Cabinet or the Parliament only during emergency.

He did not obtain the approval of the Union Cabinet or the Parliament. Therefore, *Rafale agreement* is an act of personal corruption. A product of personal corruption cannot be a constitutional one. The agreement is unconstitutional. The advocates failed to point out this to the court.

A former Judge of the Supreme Court of India, *A.K. Ganguly,* on 20 December 2018, said that the *Rafale* judgement was not based on facts present in the records. It is pertinent to recall that his 2G judgement punished former Union Minister *Mr. A. Raga* but spared his predecessor, *Mr. Arun Shourie.*

Former Attorney General of India, *Mr. Soli Sorabjee,* on 20 December 2018, said that the *Rafale* judgement must be reviewed. He does not know that it is not legally possible.

The Hindu, on 21 December 2018, quoted the following from a judgement delivered by a three-judge bench comprising Chief Justice *Ranjan Gogoi,* Justice *S.K. Kaul* and *K.M. Joseph* on December 14. 2018.

**"The perspectives of individuals may vary, but if the elected bodies which have policy formulation powers, are to be superseded by the ideals of each individual, the situation would be chaotic. The policies formulated, and the legislation made, unless they fall foul of the Constitution of India cannot be interfered with"**

If the judges know a little science, they might have said that chaos leads to stability.

**Coming to the core point, it is said that no man can obey others. In fact, if a man obeys others, it is slavery. When there is a Constitution, a man obeys the Constitution and not another man. It is the purpose of the Constitution.**

The judges also should not obey others, but they must obey the Constitution. As and when they fail to obey the Constitution, the individuals or citizens would point out the relevant sections of the Constitution to them. That is how the Constitution of India demands the citizens to protect the Constitution.

It is true that the judges must proceed with great caution while striking down an agreement, particularly when the security of the nation is treated as a facet of the case.

The Article 39 (c) states: **"that the operation of the economic system does not result in the concentration of wealth and means of production to the common detriment"**

**It is a well-defined and dominant Article consistent with the essence of the Constitution of India. Articles 38, 41, 42, 43, 45, the Preamble and may sections complement it. The Supreme Court of India has no power to supersede, add or modify it on the general considerations of supposed public interest or the security of the nation.**

**The offset clause seeks to load some people with riches using public money, that too, perennially.  Therefore, it conflicts with the above Article 39. It falls foul of the Constitution of India. The court cannot deny it.**

**The policy formulation powers of the elected Government should not supersede this Article.**

When, a citizen of India points out this to the Chief Justice India, the court should not consider it as an ideal of an individual or a perspective of an individual. It must consider it as an ideal of the Constitution of India.

**When a policy or agreement does violence to Article 39, the court must take the Constitution and reject the policy or agreement. It is the purpose of the court.**

Or the judges must openly say that they rejected this section in the context of the security of nation.

Or they must openly say in the judgement that they ignored this section in public interest.

In the passage quoted above, the three judges say, that they would reject the policy formulations of the elected Government, if they fall foul of the Constitution of India. At the same time, they justify the offset clause of the *Rafale* agreement.

**After obliterating the vital Article of the Constitution of India, the judges say that they would do everything if anything falls foul of the Constitution of India. What a conflict is it?**

**Now, due to the conflicts with Article 39 (C) the *Rafale* judgement is unconstitutional. Further, there exists conflict within the judgement and this produces absurd results.**

The judges are not expected to act in bad faith.

But they act in bad faith by projecting the criminals alone through the media.

Therefore, the Supreme Court of India must restrain the media under its jurisdiction from showing any criminals guilty of doing violence to Article 39 (a), 39(b) and 39(c) and their supporters

It must note that it sent *Mr. Laloo Prasad Yadav* and *Mrs. Sasikala* to jail for small offences. But it is doing everything possible, in very bad faith, to elect bigger criminals by suppressing the real leaders from the eye of the people.

If the Supreme Court of India wants to show any leaders through any TV channels or newspapers, under its jurisdiction, they should have done something more for nation building than the present man.

**The Supreme Court of India should not deceive the people.**

# 24

# A remiss

The public-sector TV channel, DD, as usual, on 22 December 2018, showed the leaders like Prime Minister *Mr. Narendra Modi,* former *Union P. Chidambaram.*

It must be noted that the Government of India submitted in the Supreme Court of India the decision-making process in the *Rafale* agreement. It showed that Prime Minister *Mr. Narendra Modi* did not get the approval of the Union Cabinet or the Parliament.

The working of the Government of India is a collective one. When the Parliament or the Union Cabinet is bypassed, then one must take responsibility for his acts of corruption although no prime minister would allow any minister to do anything illegal. Obviously, the Supreme Court of India alone can protect him from prosecution.

The Article 39 (C) of the Constitution of India states: **"that the operation of the economic system does not result in the concentration of wealth and means of production to the common detriment."**

The offset clause of the *Rafale* agreement allows the Government of India to transmit Re.30,000 crore in the initial stages to some people to the common detriment. The Prime Minister did it for some people for projecting him as a leader through the media and then making him a prime minister.

Evidently, the offset clause conflicts with the above Article

**Article 39(b) states; 'that the ownership and control of the material resources of the community are so distributed as best to sub serve the common good';**

This Article demands that all-natural resources must remain with the Government. They must be distributed as evenly as possible and not concentrated in a few hands. This is to give to the people of Assam, Kerala and Kashmir a reasonable share in the wealth of the nation. Therefore., all-natural resources and the privatized Public-Sector Undertakings (PSUs) must be restored forthwith and given to the States.

But Prime Minister **Mr. Narendra Modi,** just like his predecessors, alienated them even without the approval of the Parliament and the Union Cabinet. This policy conflicts with this Article. This was done for showing him in the media.

According to a ruling of the Supreme Court of India, the Government shall not pay money for publishing the image of the ministers except prime minister in the newspapers.

The newspapers and the TV channels show the images of some leaders only. They would not show anyone if it is not profitable to them.

If a man is not ready to act in conflict with Article 39, no newspaper or TV channel would publish anything about him. Thus, the corrupt alone are shown to the people.

For instance, *Mr. P. Chithambaram* had been a minister. He has been charge-sheeted for acts of corruption. Even yesterday, he got coverage in the public-sector TV channel-DD. He would share the spoils as before as and when he becomes a minister.

In contrast, the present man has acquired sufficient standing to be heard.  Yet. the TV channels black out the present man. In fact, no TV channel has uttered even a word about the present man in the last 18 years. There must be several people like the present man in India. They are being denied the chance to place their views before the people.

Thus, the corrupt are being projected as leaders and all the rest are being disqualified.

What should the present man do to be shown in the public-sector TV channel?

Should he reach an understanding with the ruling class to alienate the public resources?

**Article 39-A: directs the State to ensure that the operation of the legal system promotes justice on a basis of equal opportunity and ensure that opportunities for securing justice are not denied to any citizen.**

The Chief Justice of India proclaims that he would interfere if the policies formulated and the legislation made fall foul of the Constitution of India.

Under what policy or law does the Chief Justice of India refuse to show the present man in the public - sector TV channel? Is there any equality of opportunity?

Will it lead to chaos, if he is shown to the people?

This is not simply the cry of the present man to be heard. It is the cry 1000 million absent class citizens. The logical extension of this policy of the Chief Justice of India is that a man with 100 times better contribution for nation building than the present man would not be shown to the people tomorrow.

10 months ago, the present Chief Justice of India walked out of the court and declared that the democracy in India was in danger. Is democracy safe in his hands to-day?

The Chief Justice of India knows that he could neither correct his *Rafale* judgement as demanded by the Government nor could he recall it as demanded by the petitioners. The present man stopped everything. Hundreds of similar things happened in last 18 years. Should not the people know this? Now, even the illiterate people ask, "What happened to the *Rafale* judgement?".

The Chief Justice of India should not evade his responsibility or sacrifice his intellectual integrity. He can convene a meeting of the judges and **'yield to the common sense of the most'**.

He would be **'a remiss'** in his responsibilities as the Chief Justice of India if he were to refuse to do justice or give his opinion in this matter.

# 25

# Dispensing their own brand of justice

*Mr. Sitaram Yechuri,* a leader of the Left parties, on 24 December 2018, said that no clean chit had been given to Prime Minister of India *Mr. Narendra Modi* in the *Rafale deal* by the Supreme Court of India. According to him, the court merely stated that it did not have the jurisdiction to intervene in this matter.

The Supreme Court of India has jurisdiction over everything that comes under the jurisdiction of the Constitution of India. However, it cannot correct its own judgement.

It is true that the endeavor of the court in the *Rafale* matter was to take away the offset clause from the Constitution of India.

Why does the media report his views now? The leaders of the Left parties have been playing a complementary role to the leaders of the ruling parties to alienate the public resources. They have been helping them to wriggle out from tricky situations.

Many political leaders do violence to Articles 39 and 19. The degree would be in the following decreasing order.

Prime Minister of India *Mr. Narendra Modi* alienated the natural resources in the name of auction. He gave about Re.59000 crore in the pretext of gas subsidy. He signed an offset clause in the *Rafale* deal by doing violence to Articles 39 and 19.

'A prime minister need not be an educated person. I will prove that even an eight-standard man can run the country so long as the media is ready to strange the people. I have the privilege to modify the views of the people and use them as my own. I need not look at the files. I can issue oral orders for anything. Nobody would catch me red handed. I can take any bad faith actions and whitewash them as good faith action. I can ignore even the Union Cabinet' This is the style of functioning of Prime Minister of India *Mr. Narendra Modi.* The media gives maximum coverage to this kind of people. However, he is the only leader of this kind in India.

Next comes *Dr. Manmohan Singh* like leaders. He alienated the natural resources of India. The method adopted by him is a different one. He simply connived at their alienation buy the union ministers. Even the money in the Provident Fund and Pension Fund went to unknown places without his knowledge. He would not place important financial matters in the Union Cabinet lest someone oppose it. He would not accept responsibility for any illegal decisions taken by the ministers. There are only three or four leaders in this category.

*Mr. Arun Shourie* come under the third category of leaders. He helped privatize 34 Public Sector Undertakings (PSUs) as if it is his national duty. For this kind of leaders, fair is foul, and foul is fair. They show to the world that they are hard workers. Now, he talks like a crusader against corruption. They are not particular in maintaining a vote bank. The media gives coverage to about 20 such leaders.

The leaders of the left parties come next. They know that the Indians have no freedom. Yet, they relish it.

The exposure given to the national leaders in the media is in the above decreasing order.

A memorial of former prime minister *Mr. Atal Bihari Vajpayee* called *'Sadaiv'* was dedicated to the nation by *Prime Minister of India Mr. Narendra Modi* on 25 December 2018.

*Mr. Vajpayee* privatized 34 PSUs during his stint as the Prime Minister of India. Thus. he did violence to Article 39 of the Constitution of India. Some say that he wanted privatization, but some others say that he opposed it.

The VSNL was sold against the money taken from the Bank of India. Some others were privatized in violation of the guidelines devised for privatization.

He was the first to use the concept of Group of Ministers (GoM). The GoM could easily take many unconstitutional decisions. During his time, the Supreme Court of India was not allowed to give freedom to Indians.

*Prime Minister of India Mr. Narendra Modi,* on 25 December 2018, said that demon of corruption was becoming strong in Odessa. According to him, he is not a corrupt person, but all the rest are corrupt.

He gave Re. 30,000 crore to some people in the pretext of an offset clause while buying the *Rafale* fighter jets and agreed to give unlimited public money to them continually. This conflicts with Article 39. If the Union Cabinet or the Parliament had approved it, the Supreme Court of India could have declared the deal an unconstitutional one.

Here, he signed the offset clause, without the approval of the Union Cabinet. He had been caught red handed by the Supreme Court of India in an act of corruption.

It is true that the then Prime Minister of India- *Mr. A.B. Vajpayee* privatized 34 PSUs by doing violence to Article 39. But, no Prime Minister of India can ever commit a bigger act of corruption than this one.

But, the learned judges of India found nothing wrong in the decision-making process.

If the judges are not guilty of corruption, they might have brought to the notice of the illiterate people of India the 669 letters sent by the present man. They might have told the people that there is nothing to hide. This is not happening.

**The judges do not sit in the Supreme Court of India to dispense their own brand of justice.** They must know that their verdict is legitimate only if they draw the essence of the Constitution of India for its interpretation. They should not invoke any laws, principles or convention that conflicts with the Constitution of India for their interpretation.

The judges can give any judgement is an atmosphere of freedom. If they deny freedom and write such judgements, they cannot invoke the good faith theory. They can be tried under the anticorruption laws.

# 26

# Bombing the Rafale deal

The Economic Times, on 26 December 2018, said that **the *Rafale row* bombed a groundbreaking move** that would have changed Indian defense.

The media says that the promoters of Prime Minister of India *Mr. Narendra Modi* might have converted India into a super power, if he had been allowed to implement the offset clause of the *Rafale deal.*

Who bombed the Rafale deal?

*Mr. Arun Shourie, Yashwant Sinha* and *Prasant Bhusan* did not demand the Supreme Court of India to declare the *Rafale deal* an unconstitutional one. Instead, they wanted a probe by the *Central Bureau of Investigation (CBI).* The idea was to implements the *Rafale deal* while the case is under a *CBI* investigation. The *CBI* would cover it up is a different matter.

In this way, they would tell the people that they did everything valiantly for the people of India.

By strange luck, a Supreme Court of India bench headed by Chief Justice *Ranjan Gogoi* wanted the Government of India to submit the decision - making process in a sealed cover. Again, by strange luck, they asked the media to publish the decision- making process.

The judges concluded that there was nothing wrong in the decision-making process. The moment they failed to notice the clear and convincing evidence of wrong doing of the Prime Minister of India, *Mr. Narendra Modi*, the present man pointed out that **'a part cannot play the role of the whole'** and as such the Group of Ministers (GoM) cannot be a substitute for the Union Cabinet.

But the judges were willing to hear too much irrelevancy rather than hearing the enough of the relevant matters from the present man. Thus, no advocate was encouraged to mention Article 39 or the Union Cabinet. In fact, they did not demand the advocates to cite relevant Articles in support of their argument or discuss the consequences of not placing the *Rafale agreement* before the Union Cabinet or the Parliament or the offset clause of the *Rafale deal.* At no time, the advocates wanted the court to annul the *Rafale deal* at all.

To ensure a fair hearing, the judges should have placed the letters they received from the public in the open court and asked the advocates to point out the constitutionality or otherwise of the *Rafale deal.* They did not do so. They simply **evaded sounder reasoning.**

The above attitude indicated a lack of understanding of the judicial process.

It is pertinent to recall the words of John Day Larkin.

"That which is erroneous is sure to perish. Good remains. That which is bad will be cast off in due time. Little by little, old and out worm doctrines are undermined by the sounder reasoning of those called upon to interpret the language which the people have hammered out through long hours of patient effort to reach an agreement".

The court must interpret Articles 39 and 19 in the light of the above.

Finally, when the court was getting ready to correct the mistakes in its judgement as demanded by the Government, the present man said that the bench cannot add, correct or delete its judgement, and the court obeyed it.

The Code of Professional Responsibility does not apply to judges acting in bad faith. In this matter, the bench did not hesitate to obey this man. By obeying this man, they gave respect to the Code of Professional Responsibility.

Thus, the present man **bombed the *Rafale deal*** although the Chief Justice of India had caught the Prime Minister of India, *Mr. Narendra Modi* red handed. The people must know it. They must know it because the freedom to know it alone would make it a permanent one.

Now, no man knows what is happening in the Supreme Court of India. Did the media overtake the Supreme Court of India?

Anyone can be accused of misconduct in everyday life under one set of rules or others.

But the judges are not usually accused of misconduct. The act of concealing this work, from the eye of the people could be construed as misconduct on the part of the predecessors of the present Chief Justice of India.

No citizen of India should accuse the present Chief Justice of India of misconduct. He should not hesitate to grant freedom to the people and put right the public wrongs committed by the Supreme Court of India.

# 27

# Undue reverence to precedents

There are reports that a Union Cabinet Minister, *Mr. Nitin Gadkari,* ridiculed the Prime Minister of India, *Mr. Narendra Modi,* for losing the elections in three major states.

The ruling class might have asked him to do so. They think that Prime Minister *Mr. Modi* might not recover from three major corruption charges.1. The gas subsidy policy 2. The *Rafale offset clause* and 3. The alienation of natural assets.

Alternatively, the ruling class wants him to leave the place for exposing the money in the Reserve Bank of India (RBI) at the instance of the present man.

The ruling class can protect him from the corruption charges. But, they may not relish his moves towards the RBI.

There are reports that the Government of India issued orders to the law enforcement agencies - the Central Bureau of Investigation (CBI), Research and Analysis Wing (RAW), Directorate of Enforcement (ED) and seven others to take content from any computers of citizens.

The present Chief Justice of India might not have shared the last few letters - he received from the present man - with Prime Minister of India *Mr. Narendra Modi.* Therefore, the latter might have decided to penetrate the computers of the citizens.

In this connection, it must be stated that the present man requested the Chief Justice of India not to share the letters with others only if he cannot direct the media to publish them.

Further, the present man would reveal all letters at any time in the form of books although they may not reach the people - in general - and the illiterate people of India - in particular.

The Prime Minister of India, *Mr. Narendra Modi,* on 30 December 2018, requested the citizens to share positive news viral to know about the heroes of the nation. He added that the act of "spreading negativity is fairly easy".

He said that many people dedicated their lives for the welfare of all in society. In this connection, he mentioned the names of *Dr. Jayachandran* and *Sulagitti Narsamma.*

After converting hundreds of heroes into zeroes, he talks like this.

His speech gives the impression that the Supreme Court of India is making some feeble moves to inform the people the news and views according to degree. The media retaliates by keeping the Supreme Court of India in the *Tihar jail.*

The reason for the above conclusion is that the media has been blacking out the functioning of the Supreme Court of India for the last 15 days.

The Prime Minister of India is free to fill the Union Cabinet with his like-minded people. But he cannot bypass the Union Cabinet for taking crucial economic decisions. Therefore, the *Rafale deal* is out and out unconstitutional. It is a symbol of personal corruption

During emergency, he can ignore the Union Cabinet. But he must take the decisions in good faith only. Therefore, he can use his power to do good to the society only even during emergency.

The people believe that the public sector VSNL was privatized through a resolution of the Union Cabinet. The Supreme Court of India can declare it as an unconstitutional decision because the decision did violence to Article 39. But the court cannot punish the members of the Union Cabinet for taking such decisions.

However, if a prime minister dares to privatize a Public-Sector Undertaking (PSU) without the approval of the Union Cabinet, he is liable to be prosecuted under the Anticorruption Act or others for misusing his power.

The action of the Supreme Court of India in the *Rafale* case confirms the worst fears of the people that the prime ministers since 2001 have been taking anti-constitutional decisions on three major grounds.

Firstly, the prime minister bypasses the Union Cabinet while taking crucial economic decisions.

Secondly, his decisions conflict with Article 39.

Thirdly, to commit the above offences, he denies freedom of expression.

Therefore, the Supreme Court of India denies freedom of expression not to prevent the present man from becoming a prime minister but to promote criminality in India. In fact, the TV channels and the newspapers show the criminals only as political leaders.

When a policy of the Government conflicts with Article 39, the latter would prevail. Therefore, all privatized PSUs must be restored forthwith.

The Chief Justice of India is duty bound to take remedial measures.

If he refuses to do his duty, he also becomes a criminal. Why should a chief justice of India become a criminal?

The Chief Justice of India shall not refuse to do his duty just because his predecessors chose not to do their duty. He shall not give **undue reverence to precedents** when a prime minister does violence to the Constitution of India.

The Chief Justice of India derives his power from the Constitution of India, and he has no authority to invoke any laws, conventions, principles, policies or precedents that conflict with the Constitution of India.

# 28

# The fear of reprisals

There are reports that the first batch of *Rafale* fighter jets would land in India within days.

The Government of India can buy or sell anything consistent with the Constitution of India. But it cannot do anything in violation of the Constitution of India.

The *Rafale deal* conflicts with Article 39 of the Constitution of India.

The deal was signed without the approval of the Union Cabinet. This is against the Constitution of India.

To commit the above offences, the Supreme Court of India keeps the letters from the present man away from the eye of the people. This is also unconstitutional.

Therefore, it should restrain the Government of India from buying the *Rafale* jets based on the *Rafale* judgement.

The petitioners in the *Rafale* case did not demand the court to consider the constitutionality or otherwise of the *Rafale* deal. The case was purely for a probe into the alleged acts of corruption. Therefore, that judgement is not the seal of the court to buy the jets as per the *Rafale* deal.

The judges of the Supreme Court of India need not be experts in law to understand the contentions of the present man.

They must use the **"reasonable man standard"** to dispose the letters of the present man.

**They must know that the general principles do not decide concreate cases.**

Several concrete cases have been brought to the notice of the Chief Justice of India through 672 letters. The court has not given any reply.

The Chief Justice of India is immune from civil liability for acts done in his official capacity. But he must be free from **the fear of reprisals** and he must be uninfluenced by any fear of consequences for his acts.

The Chief Justice of India wanted everything in sealed covers. Now the media is keeping the Supreme Court of India in a sealed cover. They don't allow him to give even a reply to 672 letters.

Evidently, he does not give a reply to 672 letters because of **the fear of reprisals** and consequences.

He must do his duty to the nation without the fear of reprisals and consequences.

It must be recalled that Justice *Ranjan Gogoi*, before assuming office as the Chief Justice of India said, "The public interest litigation (PIL) are for the poor. Anyone could knock at the door of the Supreme Court of India for justice".

The present man is knocking at the doors of the Supreme Court of India for the 673 rd time.

# 29

# Criminalizing Indian elections

The Prime Minister of India, *Mr. Narendra Modi*, on 1 January 2019, gave his answers to some tutored questions of a reporter. This was his first interview after assuming power as the Prime Minister of India - four and a half years ago.

The questions and the readymade answers give the impression that the present Chief Justice of India *Ranjan Gogoi* shared the contents of the 28 letters he received from the present man with Prime Minister *Mr. Modi*. Alternatively, the Government might have intercepted the emails.

To a question the Prime Minister said, *"I could not win over the "Lutyen's World". I am still trying to win over such forces. I am a representative of the non-elite world. There is honesty in my work"*

What does he mean by "Lutyen's World" cannot be deciphered?

He concealed 645 letters of the present man from the eye of the people. Yet, he claims that there is honesty in his ways.

To another question, he said, "The leaders who want to loot the nation are closing ranks and forming alliances"

He alienated the public resources. He gave Re. 59,000 crore to his promoters in the pretext of gas subsidy. He agreed to pay a tribute of Re. 30,000 crore as the first instalment of an offset clause.to the ruling class. He did everything by doing violence to Article 39 of the Constitution of India- without even placing them in the Union Cabinet. In this way, he turned the Constitution of India upside down in very bad faith.

Yet he says that the leaders of the opposition parties want to loot the nation!

*When an Article or a section of a Constitution is not consistent with its essence, the people might approach the competent court for its interpretation. When there is nothing ambiguous in a section of a Constitution, there is no need for any interpretation.*

The words of the Article 39 of the Constitution of India are plain, clear conveying a distinct idea. Therefore, the Supreme Court of India need not resort to technical interpretations or invoke the chaos theory but must apply it in a straightforward manner. Ordinarily, the judges in many countries apply such provisions as part of their divine duty and leave the place.

There can be occasions when a provision is clear and definite, yet the result of the whole is doubtful. During such occasions, freedom could be given to the people to debate the matter until the judges get a clear idea.

Now, the act of concealing the essential facts and the act of distorting the truth give the impression that the Supreme Court of India exists to promote the people habitually doing violence to Article 39 of the Constitution of India. The judges simply describe peace and order as Justice, and freedom as chaos.

In fact, the TV channels and the newspapers show the offenders of Article 39 only to the people. **Thus, the Chief Justice of India criminalizes Indian politics, rigs the elections and installs illegitimate governments.**

# 30

# Promiscuous enforcement

Advocate *Prasant Bhusan*, the advocate for the petitioners in the *Rafale case,* on 2-1-2019, moved a review petition before the Supreme Court of India.

The media had been keeping the Supreme Court of India in a sealed cover since the *Rafale judgement.*

This is the first time the media is reporting the functioning of the Supreme Court of India after the *Rafale judgement.*

Now, the media has sparingly reported the case. It has not mentioned the judges in the present bench.

Immediately after the *Rafale judgement,* the Government of India sought a correction in the judgement. But, *Mr. Prasant Bhuson* wanted the court to recall the judgement because of the factual errors.

The present man immediately pointed out that the judges cannot add, delete, modify or correct a judgement.

Therefore, at the instance of the Prime Minister of India, the petitioners and the Attorney General of India met Chief Justice of India *Ranjan Gogoi* at his chamber and devised a strategy, in bad faith, to annul the effects of the letters from the present man. The Chief Justice then instructed the media to report the matter sparingly only. He asked it not to report the names of the judges in the bench to the people.

However, the present man knows his letters and the present condition. What happened in between - during the 17 days - is an imagination only. If he does not publish the letters, one would tell that he is part of a bad faith conspiracy to rig the impending elections.

Whatever happened, **the Supreme Court of India is forbidden from enforcing anything promiscuously.** This is the legal position, But the judges acting in good faith alone would obey it.

# 31

# Class Action Suit

The Supreme Court of India, on 3-1-2019, revived a class-action suit by the central government against the *Nestle* company in the National Consumer Disputes and Redressal Commission (NCDRC). The Government of India had sought compensation of Re.640 crore under the provisions of the Consumer Protection Act, 1986 for the alleged unfair trade practices.

The loss suffered by a citizen of India due to the alleged unfair trade practices of the *Nestle* may be very small. But the combined loss to all citizens may be very large.

A citizen of India cannot file a case and pursue it in courts because of the small amount suffered by him.

It is customary in the USA for a citizen to file a class action suit. However, any affected citizen cannot file such a suit. The essential condition is that the petitioner must have a **standing** in the society. This condition would prevent frivolous suits.

In the above suit, the Government of India represents the citizen with the requisite standing.

In a democracy, a citizen aspiring to become a prime minister must place his record of public activities before the people as in a market place. The customers- the people - are free to select their prime ministerial candidate. This is the concept of democracy by many political philosophers like Holmes.

For the above, 'the constitution limits the majority and protects the minority usually through the enjoyment by all of certain individual rights eg freedom of speech or freedom of association'

There must be an absence of government involvement in ensuring freedom of speech. Then only the elections will be free.

The present man has sent 676 letters for freedom and wellbeing of the people; and hundreds of changes have taken place in the last 18 years, Had the Supreme Court of India allowed the present man to place his activities before the people, *Dr. Manmohan Singh* might not have become a prime minister at all. The people might have chosen a man like the present man as their prime minister.

All public resources might have come under the control of the Government consistent with Article 39 of the Constitution of India. The Public - Sector Undertakings might have been split and handed over to the States. Every media institution might have come under one or more voluntary organizations and the people might have got a chance to know news and views according to degree. The people might have chosen the best available candidates. They might have seen freedom.

Therefore, the paramount duty of the Supreme Court of India is to enlarge freedom by limiting the power of the majority. The court need not listen to the Government in this matter at all. It should not compromise freedom on any ground.

However, it has not happened. The court shows the criminals only to the people, Consequently, 'the loss suffered by a citizen may be small, but the principle is very large'

Therefore, the Chief Justice of India is liable for class action suit. The present man has the requisite standing to file a suit. In India, the procedure is impeachment. It is not easy.

Why should a man occupy the place of the Chief Justice of India, if he cannot enforce freedom of expression? Is he an ordinary person to sit like this?

The Chief Justice of India would say, that a person might pursue his self - interest. But it is said that **'when an individual pursues his self-interest under conditions of justice, he unintentionally promotes the good of society'.**

But the tragedy is that even the present Chief Justice of India robs the people of their freedom just to deprive them of their properties.

# 32

# Producing illegitimate governments

The Supreme Court of India, on 3 January 2019, said that the bench for the *Ramjamabhoomi- Babri Masjid title suit* is to be announced on 10 January 2018.

The circumstances that led to the sudden announcement must be noticed.

A Hindu religious organization, VHP, had exhorted the ruling BJP to impeach the Chief Justice of India for the delay in taking the title suit for hearing. Then, the Prime Minister of India, *Mr. Narendra Modi,* accused the Chief Justice of India of obstructing justice in this matter. The present man – in another context - had also requested him to do his divine duty and leave the place.

Therefore, when the matter was brought before *Chief Justice Ranjan Gogoi,* he took just 30 seconds to announce his decision to constitute a bench by January 10, 2019. He did not listen to the arguments of the advocates.

Now, the Chief Justice of India can grant freedom to the people. He would need just 30 seconds to announce it.

The majority – the Members of Parliament, the political leaders, the law enforcing agencies and the media mafias closed ranks long ago to rob freedom.

The present man has the requisite standing to become the Prime Minister of India. But he has been injured by the continuing illegal activity of the majority – the Supreme Court of India included.

The Chief Justices of India since June 2001 have been taking an interest in maintaining this illegal activity.

Under these conditions, it is very easy for any prime minister to strange the views of his antagonists.

It is the vital duty of the Supreme Court of India to impose a limitation on the illegal activity of the majority. If it is not done, the minority could never seek the votes of the impartial people.

The Chief Justice of India should not consider it as an individual issue because this is happening to all citizens of India.

Is it possible for the Chief Justice of India to give democracy to Indians?

Yes. It is a possible one. In fact, he can accomplish it in 30 seconds.

For it, he must direct the media to tell the illiterate people of India the salient features of the letters received by him after assuming power as the Chief Justice of India.

Then, the people would reject the criminals and elect a man from the minority as a prime minister in the 2019 General Elections.

The present man has a fair chance of becoming a prime minister because the people would examine what one did to the nation rather than what one would do after winning an election.

Otherwise, the No.1 criminal of India will seize power producing an illegitimate government.

# 33

# The nodal point

The Central Bureau of Investigation (CBI) Joint Director *Mr. Murugesan* was, on 5 January 2019, substituted by *Mr. G.K. Goswami,* Joint Director of Lucknow zone. *Mr. Goswami* will probe the corruption charges levelled against Special CBI Director *Rakesh Asthana* by Director *Alok Varma.*

When the Government divested the duties of *Mr. Alok Varma* and *Mr. Asthana* simultaneously, a new team led by Joint Director *Mr.Murugesan* was constituted by the Government. The other members of the team under *Mr. Murugesan* were not disturbed.

Even literate people have no time to bother about the above case. In fact, the Chief Justice of India rejects this case as something not necessary for the growth of people.

If Chief Justice of India *Ranjan Gogoi* is not ready to grant freedom, an impartial observer would say that **he carried out certain**

**things promiscuously and applied a corrupt man standard to judge the case.** Therefore, an atmosphere of freedom is essential to take the best out of the judges like him.

The purpose of sending letters continuously for 18 years is to fully inform the Chief Justice of India the nature of the problem staring at India so that relief might be available - one day or other- provided the demand is a constitutional one.

As this work has progressed to 678 letters, the Chief Justice of India has no difficulty in discerning the precise issue.

The Chief Justice of India need not demand the citizens any formal pleadings like the one frequently used by *Mr. Prasant Bhusan* like advocates to determine the precise issue to be resolved. Such pleadings would destroy some of the simplicity and utility of the Constitution of India as is evident from the *Rafale* case.

But a citizen of India must pinpoint the issue to be resolved by the Chief Justice of India. The present citizen relies on the word or clause or suggestion in the Constitution of India that **'You'** alone can protect the Constitution of India. The word  **'You'** could be the Chief Justice of India, any one of the judges of the Supreme Court of India, a prime minister, a president, or a citizen of India like the present man.

But experience shows that if the Chief Justice of India stands on the way, in bad faith, no citizen of India could protect it.

Therefore, it is imperative that the Chief Justice of India must use the word **'You'** in a logical manner consistent with the language and intent of the Constitution. 'He should not construe the Constitution narrowly and technically but broadly to accomplish its evident aims'.

It is not within the function of the Chief Justice of India to look outside the Constitution to carry out the agenda of any man or a class of people and describe as constitutional. Instead, his sole duty is find out what was meant by the language of the Constitution.

If the language of the Constitution demands that he must inform the letters to the people for their freedom of thought, he should not hesitate to do that.

The present Chief Justice of India now knows that some people sitting away from the scene of action run the country through the aid of the Chief Justice of India and some hardened criminals. Their media wing tells the people that the ballot paper decides the outcome of the elections. But they do not allow the people to know men and matters. They do this to plunder the public resources.

**The nodal point is the Chief Justice of India because the people sitting away from the scene of action act through the Chief Justice of India.**

The people plundering the nation – called the ruling class- demand the Chief Justice of India not to tell the illiterate people of India the nature of the letters he receives from the people. In contrast, the people opposing this plunder request him to tell the illiterate people the nature of the letters he receive from the citizens.

The present Chief Justice of India is fully conscious of both the forces.

Usually, a man gets a chance to become a Chief Justice of India only after reaching an understanding with the ruling class. The present Chief Justice of India can tell whether he reached an understanding with them or not to become the Chief Justice of India.

It is pertinent to recall that Justice *Ranjan Gogoi* came out of the Supreme Court of India with three others, on 12 January 2018, and said that the then Chief Justice of India, *Dipak Misra*, was remotely controlled and that democracy in India was in danger.

Thus, he described the then Chief Justice of India as the No.1 criminal among the public servants in India. All other public servants would come below him in the public servant-criminal series. The series would be in the following decreasing order.

The Chief Justice of India > judges of the Supreme Court of India > The Prime Minister of India > The President of India > Union Cabinet Ministers > Heads of law enforcing agencies like the CBI >The Chief Justices of High Courts.

There is a reason for arriving at the above series. The statement of Justice Holmes that, "it is not adequate discharge of duty for courts to say, we see what you are driving at, but you have not said it and, therefore, we shall go on as before"

If the Chief Justice of India continues to be the Number 1 criminal, he cannot publish the letters received by him in his capacity as the Chief Justice of India.

Otherwise, he would release the letters to the media for the freedom of Indians.

Therefore, the issue is freedom.

If the people get freedom, they might choose the present citizen as the Prime Minister of India. Otherwise, the present unconstitutional set up would continue.

The Chief Justice of India is confronting an issue growing out of a situation envisaged by the founding fathers of the Constitution of India only. If he wants to act in good faith, he can solve it within 30 seconds.

The rule of Constitution demands the publication of the letters.

# 34

# 'To thine own self be true'

The Prime Minister of India, *Mr. Narendra Modi,* on 6 January 2019, said that *Mr. Chandra Babu Naidu* was day -dreaming to become the Prime Minister of India.

Prime Minister *Mr. Narendra Modi* might have intercepted the emails sent to the Chief Justice of India or the latter might have shared the contents of the emails with him.

What he meant by *Chandra Babu Naidu* is *Sabarimuthu* – the present citizen of India.

It is true that the people would choose the present man as their prime minister, if they get a chance to understand the salient points of the 680 letters.

But Prime Minister *Mr. Narendra Modi* would not grant freedom to the illiterate people of India to know the contribution of the present man for their wellbeing.

In fact, no prime minister anywhere in the world would give freedom to the people to know his antagonist. The reason is simple. The prime ministers possess the power to deny freedom. So long as he possesses this power, he would continue to deny freedom. However, it is illegal.

A newspaper, on the same day, asked the people through an article whether the Leader of the Opposition and Congress President *Mr. Rahul Gandhi* could lead the Congress Party to a national win.

A few articles like this one on the present man would easily make him the Prime Minister of India.

The newspapers and the TV channels select a man for the post of the Prime Minister of India.

They have the power to do this. So long as they possess this, they would not show their enemies to the people.

Thus, experience shows that the Government and the media mafia possess the power to take away the freedom of the people to know men and matters. The law enforcing agencies and the Election Commission of India (ECI) play a complementary role to deprive the people of their freedom.

To prevent the Government, opposition parties and the media mafia from doing the above, the Constitution of India imposes some limitations on their power.

Thus, the Constitution allows them to do anything other than denying freedom to the citizens.

The Constitution is very harsh in this matter.

Thus, if the Government wants Electronic Voting Machines (EVM), the ECI can say that the voting must be through ballot paper.

Even the court cannot interfere in the decisions taken by it in good faith. It can maintain an atmosphere of freedom. It can allot timings for canvassing in the TV channels. It can impose conditions on the media to report men and matters as per degree.

Similarly, the prime Minister of India can do anything other than taking away the freedom of the people. He cannot direct the media to conceal the letters of the people with the requisite standing. The Constitution demands the Supreme Court of India to limits its power to deny freedom.

As the Supreme Court of India acts in bad faith, he mis-uses his power and takes away the freedom of the people.

He and other political leaders now get 24 hours coverage in the TV channels. The newspapers also mention their words and deeds daily. They have political parties and mass support. They have unlimited money also.

The present man possesses none of the above. Yet he says that the people would choose him as the Prime Minister of India.

Therefore, the Chief Justice of India must release the letters he received from the present man and direct the media to give 5 per cent coverage to the letters. In this matter, he can take the opinion of the other judges.

The Chief Justice of India is free to relay on the background of his experience or expertise to provide as practical and realistic an interpretation as is possible under the Constitution of India. But he cannot say that he lacks the necessary expertise to write a judgement as in the *Rafale* case. He cannot say that he lacks enough knowledge to determine the constitutionality or otherwise of an offset clause. He cannot refuse to enforce freedom of expression in India. Above all, he cannot say that he does not understand the meaning of the letters.

The function of the Chief Justice of India is not to make the Constitution of India a defunct one or to rewrite it. If he believes that the Constitution of India contains inequities, he should not use his sense of justice and fairness but must use the essence of the Constitution of India to judge the issues.

'Prime Minister *Mr. Modi* promoted me. I must be loyal to him. My father is a Congress man. I must return the debt to *Mr. Rahul Gandhi*". No chief justice shall talk like this.

Should a Chief Justice reckon the economic consequences of his judgement?

No. The economic consequences should not influence him in his ultimate decision.

Thus, he should not have allowed the Government to do violence to Article 39.

The Chief Justice must take the essence from the Constitution of India and tell the Government unequivocally what it can or cannot do inside the Constitution of India.

The Chief Justice of India should not conceal the letters from the eye of the people because the Constitution of India limits his power to do this.

It is customary for the legal educators to quote from Shakespeare. *"And this above all; to thine own self be true, and it must follow as the night the day. Thou canst then be false to anyone"*. By 'false', *Polonius* says that a man should not do anything disadvantageous or detrimental to his own image. By 'true' he means "loyal to own best interests". Take care of yourself first, he counsels, and that way you will be able to take care of others.

If the Chief Justice of India does something detrimental to his own image, 1300 million people would be affected.

# 35

# The restrictive clauses

The email sent to the Chief Justice of India yesterday (7-1-20018) was intercepted by the Government. Alternatively, the Chief Justice of India shared it with the Government of India.

The reason for the above conclusion is that the Prime Minister of India convened a meeting of the Union Cabinet immediately after the email. The Cabinet decided to grant 10 per cent reservation to the poor among the Forward Communities.

The Forward Communities constitute less than ten per cent of the population. A caste-based census is needed to determine this quota.

The above decision was given great publicity, only to divert the attention of the people to other matters.

However, the Cabinet turned down the request of the present man to grant freedom to Indians.

"You must obey what we say. Don't we give food and water to you? Is it not enough? We have granted freedom to all. That is why you talk whatever you want in the tea shop. You can write anything to us. But the air waves belong to us. We won't let the people to know what you do. We can even strange the Supreme Court of India. We won't allow the citizens to know men and matters. No citizen -unless he is our hired man- can aspire to rule us. This is our decree. This is the essence of the Constitution of India".

Anyone can discern the nature of Indian elections and the Government.

Curiously, the Union Cabinet is taking some policy decisions. For the offset clause of the *Rafale* deal, the Cabinet was not consulted. To privatize the Public-Sector Undertakings (PSUs), the Cabinet was not taken into confidence. Perhaps the Prime Minister *Mr. Modi* understands the meaning of the Cabinet System of Government now.

A Supreme Court of India bench comprising Chief Justice of India *Ranjan Gogoi*, Justice *Joseph* and Justice *Kaul,* on 8 January 2019, reinstated *Mr. Alok Varma* as the Director of Central Bureau of Investigation (CBI). However, the court barred him from taking any policy decisions. The bench added that the selection panel will meet within a week to take a decision on the corruption charges leveled against him by former Additional Director of the CBI *Mr. Rakesh Asthana.*

It must be noted that the present man sent over 250 letters to the CBI, CVC, NHRC, judges of the Supreme Court of India and the Chief Justices of the High Courts.

Some Chief Justices of India, some judges of the Supreme Court of India and the Chief Justices of High Courts might have referred many letters to the CBI for necessary action because the letters contained many complaints against many public servants, particularly political leaders and the judges.

CBI Director *Mr. Alok Varma* might have noticed them in the files. He might have intercepted the emails also. But he did not do his duty.

Therefore, the assertion that he was free from political interference cannot be accepted.

The reason for the above conclusion is that no judge – unless he is a corrupt man – would bury the complaints against public servants in the court.

Many people now think that the Chief Justice of India applied *'a reasonable man standard'* to judge the case.

However, if he had received any bribe, he should have been arrested just like other public servants. Otherwise, he should have been reinstated with full liberty of action.

Further, how can there be reinstatement without any decision-making power? There exists a conflict within the judgement.

Furthermore, Prime Minister's Office (PMO) had asked *Mr. Alok Varma* to pursue the cases against *Mr. Lalu Prasad Yadav* - a powerful political leader. The message was that the Prime Minister of India asked him to keep *Mr. Lalu Prasad Yadav* in jail until his death. The Prime Minister and the PMO did not deny it. Can *Mr. Alok Varma* take this case now? Nothing is clear.

Curiously, Chief Justice of India *Ranjan Gogoi* did not attend the court to deliver the judgement. There is no news about any leave either

Chief Justice of India *Ranjan Gogoi* is full of remorse for not disclosing the contents of the letters. He thinks that his action is detrimental to his interests. Therefore, he chose to hide his feelings.

Everyone commits mistakes. Chief Justice *Ranjan Gogoi* cannot be an exception. When the Chief Justice of India commits a mistake, it must be multiplied into 1300 million.

Article 19 of the Constitution of India states that all citizens shall have the right to freedom of speech and expression.

The perception among the judges is that the freedom of expression has some reasonable restrictions.

*'Ordinarily, all words used in a Constitution should be given effect. The fact that a word is used indicates that the founding fathers intended to have some meaning and it will not be declared surplusage if a reasonable meaning can be given to it consistent with the rest of the Constitution.''*

*However, 'it is axiomatic in the construction of a Constitution that an interpretation which tends to nullify or render meaningless any part of the Constitution should be avoided because of the general presumption that the founding fathers did not carefully write into solemnly discussed Constitution words intended to have no effect.'*

**The message is that before the words - freedom of speech and democracy - the restrictive clauses have no significance,**

***In 2002, the Union of India Vs Democratic Reforms, a Constitutional bench of the Supreme Court of India said that one sided information, disinformation, misinformation and non-information equally create an uninformed citizenry which makes democracy a farce.***

The Constitution of India demands that the Chief Justice of India must inform the salient points of the letters he received - in his official capacity - to the citizens. The judgment of the Supreme Court of India also demands the same.

The Chief Justice of India could tell the people the reason for keeping the people as mere animals for the last 18 years by concealing the letters.

There are about 135 days left for the present Union Government, A minimum of 100 days is required to form a party called Democratic Party of India. Election rules will have to be modified to accommodate this party. There must be an inner party election to elect District level,

Parliamentary Constituency level, Assembly Constituency level, State level and National level office bearers.

If the Chief Justice of India procrastinates to take a decision, the present man will not get any time.

Therefore, the Chief Justice of India is requested to start telling the outstanding futures of the letters to the illiterate people of India from tomorrow (9-1-2019) onwards.

# 36

# A farce

A Chief Justice of India *Ranjan Gogoi* -led Constitution Bench would determine the *Ayodhya title suit*. The court announced it on 8 January 2019. The bench would start the hearing on 10 January 2019.

Chief Justice *Ranjan Gogoi*, constituted the bench in such a way so that the four other judges would be future chief justices in line of seniority. They are *Justices S.A. Bobde, N.V.Ramana, U.U. Lalit* and *D.Y. Chandra Chud.*

When the High Court gave its verdict, no law and order problem occurred. Let the judges of the Supreme Court also use their talents in this matter.

'The language of the Constitution of India expresses the intent of its founding fathers.

No section or portion of it should be isolated from the rest and given constructions independently of its purpose.

The meaning of each paragraph and each sentence must be determined in relation to the Constitution as a whole'.

As every party in the suit would take advantage of the verdict, the bench must first give freedom to Indians. The reason is freedom alone would take the best from the judges.

If it is not done, the people would not get justice at all and they would begin to suspect the judges in the present bench.

To dispel the darkness, the five judges must give a decree that in future a person will become the Chief Justice of India strictly based on the date of birth seniority. This will give the impression that the judges have no private interests. This is to prevent the unwanted interferences in the judiciary by others.

The Government of Tamil Nadu had taken a decision to give Re. 1000/- per ration card to celebrate the *Pongal* festival that falls on January 14. The Madras High Court, today (on 9 January 2019), stayed it saying that it must be given to the below poverty line people only. It advised the Government to use the money for public investment. Some people say that it is gratis to influence the voters.

However, when the public sector VSNL was given to Tata, the court considered it as economic policy and refused to interfere.

Thus, at one time the court says something is economic policy and at another time it says that it is free to review anything. The conflict could be discerned.

There are reports that the CBI Director, *Mr. Alok Varma* would revoke the transfer orders affected by his substitute, *Mr.Nageswara Rao.*

If it is true, the order issued by the Supreme Court of India yesterday is reinstatement. It is a good faith action by the Chief Justice of India. The CBI is now free to release the letters of the present man to the media along with an action taken report.

However, the Chief Justice of India could have initiated a debate in the media over the 681 letters. At least, he could have informed the contents of Letter No.681 to the media. As the chief justices do not give a reply, it must be inferred that they fully concur with the views of the present man.

As early as in 2001, the learned judges of the Supreme Court of India wanted the Government and the media to disclose the letter No.1 dated 1-6-2001. The then President of India, *Mr. K.R. Narayanan,* went to the Supreme Court of India. His successor, *Dr. A.P.J. Abdul Kalam* followed suit. The media said that no mud would be allowed to stick on the then Prime Minister of India, *Mr. A.B. Vajpayee.* They even threatened to eliminate the present man. Instead of proceeding against the media mafia, the learned judges of the court described the Indian democracy as **a farce.** They gave expression to their feelings through a judgement in 2002.

After 16 years, Justice *Ranjan Gogoi* along with three others came out of the Supreme Court of India and disclosed that the then Chief Justice of India was remotely controlled, and that democracy was not safe in his hand.

The present Director of the CBI, *Mr. Alok Varma,* had disclosed that the Prime Minister's Office (PMO) wanted him to pursue some cases against *Mr. Lalu Prasad Yadav.* Will any prime minister stoop to this level? No doubt, he pokes his nose in all unwanted places and he has no time to listen to reasoned opinions.

The present man did not use harsh words - as used by the judges and the CBI Director - against anyone in the last 681 letters.

Therefore, there is no reason for the Chief Justice of India to conceal the letters from the eye of the people.

The non - information of the last letter to the people has the effect of protecting the Prime Minister of India from the charges levelled against him by the CBI Director, *Mr. Alok Varma*. Otherwise, he might have resigned by now.

If the Chief Justice of India takes time to disclose the truth to the people, the date of election will have to be changed accordingly to accommodate the present citizen.

If the media had refused to publish the letters, the Chief Justice of India should have proceeded against it.

# 37

# Representing the absent class citizens

A five judge Constitution Bench, headed by Chief Justice of India *Ranjan Gogoi,* on 10 January 2018 started the hearing of *Ayodhya temple title suit*

*Justice U.U. Lalit* recused himself from the case because of the conflict of interests. He had functioned as a lawyer for *Mr. Kalyan Singh,* former Chief Minister of Utter Pradesh, in a related case.

Chief Justice of India *Ranjan Gogoi* must recognize the simple fact that all written constitutions are interpreted by the same general principles.

It is said that the constitutions are aids to the finding of intent, not hard and fast rule to be used to defeat content.

The learned judges of the Supreme Court of India should not make any attempt to rewrite the Constitution of India by the   substitution of their views under the guise of interpretation.

This is happening occasionally.  The BALCO judgement and even the *Rafale offset clause* interpretation are examples.

In the CBI Director *Alok Varma* case, the court took an intermediate approach due to the relentless pressure from the present man.

The judges are human beings.  Regardless of the approach taken, it can be expected that the personality of the judge would creep into the judgement. After all, the judgements are the verdict of the judges and not that of somebody else.

The personality of the human beings is affected by the environment. A man does one thing under sun light. The same man does another thing at night. The probability of committing a mistake or error is greater under darkness. This is a limitation imposed by the nature,

Therefore, the learned judges would write reasonable judgements only in an atmosphere of freedom.

After the *Rafale* judgement, the defendant-, the Government- wanted to correct the judgement. The plaintiff -the petitioners - wanted to recall it. The present man asked the Chief Justice not to touch it and the latter obeyed. Otherwise, he might have committed one more mistake to his credit.

The judges would agree that the letter had the desired effect in that matter.    If the Supreme Court of India had enforced freedom of expression, the effect will have to be multiplied by 1300 million.

The message is that the letters are written not to educate the judges alone but to enlighten the 1300 million people. Just imagine the loss incurred by the people!

Therefore, the judges should not have concealed the letters even for a day.

The Prime Minister of India, *Mr. Narendra Modi,* today, January 9, 2019, said that Congress culture is corruption. He can talk like this because the Supreme Court of India does not inform the contents of the letters to the illiterate people of India.

The high-power committee comprising Chief Justice of India *Ranjan Gogoi.* Prime Minister of India *Mr. Narendra Modi* and the leader of opposition in the Lok Sabha (Lower House), *Mr. Mallikarjun Kharge* met yesterday to take a decision on the complaint against CBI Director *Mr. Alok Varma.*

The Chief Justice of India sent *Justice A.K. Sikri* to represent him in the meeting. The meeting remained inconclusive.

The Chief Justice might have discerned a conflict in the matter.

The present man, in one of the letters had given an option to him to function as a life-time judge. He might have seen a conflict in disposing the letters of the present man. Therefore, he might have asked *Justice Sikri* to represent him.

The above conclusion is an imagination only. What the present man knows is the letters sent to him and the above development.

The Prime Minister of India-led above committee, today (10-1-2019) decided to remove *Mr. Alok Varma* from the post of Director, CBI on charges of corruption and for not proceeding against *Mr. Lalu Prasad Yadav*, a political leader from Bihar and former Railway Minister.

The public -sector TV channel said that Prime Minister *Mr. Narendra Modi* and *Justice Sikri* supported the decision and Leader of the Opposition *Mr. Mallikarjun Kharge* opposed it.

As *Mr. Alok Varma* was not arrested for receiving any bribe, an impartial observer would think that he is removed from office for levelling charges against the Prime Minister's Office (PMO).

If he had received any money from anyone, he should have been arrested. Why does the Supreme Court of India protect him?

Ordinarily, a judge would construe the charges levelled against the PMO as an attempt to murder a political leader. If his charges are false, he should have arrested for that also. Why does the Supreme Court of India protect him?

All right-thinking people would suspect a conspiracy, if he is not arrested immediately.

The Supreme Court of India has been concealing the letters from the people partly to plunder the public resources and partly to deny the political rights of the citizens of India.

Now, it is concealing the letters to protect the PMO from an attempt to murder case. Does the court consider it as a good culture? Is it not detrimental to the image of the Supreme Court of India?

The Chief Justice of India can ask other judges to dispose of the letters he received from the present man if he notices any conflict of interests. They must decide whether the present man **fairly and adequately represents the 1300 million absent class citizens or not.**

# 38

# The Prime Minister of India

*Mr. Prasant Bhuson*, the advocate for the petitioners in the *Rafale* case, on 9 January 2019, used the word 'absurd' to describe the *Rafale* judgement.

The present man used this word in one of the letters submitted to the Chief Justice of India. The present man did not send that letter to anyone other than the Chief Justice of India. Perhaps, it may be his word to describe the judgement. But, why did he not press for recalling the judgement? What happened to the correction petition by the Government? Does the Chief Justice of India share the letters with others without informing that to the people?

A committee of the Election Commission of India (ECI) submitted its report for regulating the digital media.

The ECI must tell the reason for conducting elections without enforcing freedom of expression. It must tell the reason for conducting elections by Electronic Voting Machines (EVMs) rather than by ballot paper.

The Central Bureau Investigation (CBI) Director, *Mr. Alok Varma* today, on 10 January 2019, resigned from service.

*Mr. Alok Varma* is an employee - a public servant. He must be ready to work in any place. He cannot claim reinstatement in his personal capacity. He can approach the court only if the transfer is illegal. He says that he was transferred for upholding rule of law. If the Supreme Court of India does not want rule of law, an employee cannot do anything. He cannot spend money from his pocket to seek remedy from any court. At best, he can write letters to the competent authorities and leave the matter there. Therefore, he must consider it as an occupational hazard, join duty and reveal his experiences and the bad faith orders issued to him. It might go down as a great service to the nation

However, *Mr. Alok Varma* chose to resign today. He says that natural rights were scuttled as he was not given a hearing.

Natural Rights are rights that existed before the Constitution of India. He may be right in his stand.

It must be stated that the CBI lost its credibility long ago. It did not dispose of over 250 letters. At one time, it refused to accept the letters. Then the present man decided not to give any problem to the Indian Police Service (IPS) officers.

The crucial question before the Supreme Court of India is to see whether the removal of *Mr. Alok Varma* is constitutional or not.

It is the right of the appointing authority to offer employment upon its own terms.

The Supreme Court of India directed the Government to give two years to every Director. If it is not in conflict with the Constitution of India and any other judgement, the appointing authority must obey it. In fact, it is his statutory right to continue in office for two years because of the order of the Supreme Court of India. The people believe that the court gave it largely and directly in the interest of the public.

This does not mean that the Director could receive bribe from anyone. The act of accepting bribe is against the essence of the Constitution of India and it is a cognizable offence.

If there is an allegation of corruption against him, other law enforcing agencies must investigate it. If there is a reasonable suspicion, he must be suspended and arrested. No mercy need be given to him because many employees remain in jail even for accepting tips.

However, to remove his statutory rights, the order of the appointing authority must be a clear and unmistakable one. In the *Alok Varma* case, the Chief Vigilance Commissioner (CVC) said that there was no direct evidence of corruption. No First Information Report (FIR) was filed.

Therefore, all right-thinking people think that there is breach of contractual protection. It is improper for the committee to club the main charges with others. In fact, the Supreme Court of India has not developed any statutory principles for evaluating the general circumstances behind the main issue. The order against *Mr. Alok Varma* conflicts with the published policies of the Supreme Court of India and the general perception of the people. The people think that it is against the interest of the public.

The Constitution of India does not permit the appointing committee to take unilateral decision because the appointing authority's right to take such actions is not clearly and unmistakably spelled out in the appointment order, if any, served to *Mr. Alok Varma* or in the order of the court.

When the Supreme Court of India remains as a parasite to take away the political rights of 1300 people, the CBI cannot be an independent institution and such things are bound to happen.

Another serious charge was that he refused to proceed against *Mr. Lalu Prasad Yadav*, former Chief Minister of Bihar and former Railway Minister.

*Wikileaks* had revealed that *Mr. Lalu Prasad Yadav*, just like many other Indian political leaders, had kept a huge amount of money -over Re.10,000 crore in the Swiss banks. The Supreme Court of India alone knows the veracity of the leaks.

*Mr. Lalu Prasad Yadav* is a leader in the Bihar State thanks to the local media. He is not an all India leader because the media mafia did not want him. Anyhow, he is a mass leader.

There are hundreds of cases against him.  He was sent to jail for Re.42 lakh because someone apparently removed money from a treasury.

Thousands of cases are going on in the courts for economic offences all over India. The public sector HZL was given to a charge sheeted company in violation the guidelines devised for privatization. No action was taken.

Under these situations, the Prime Minister of India could have directed the CBI to proceed against all offenders according degree. To be on the safer side, he could have passed a resolution in the Union Cabinet.

Here, the Prime Minister's Office (PMO) directed the CBI Director to proceed against him in other cases. It is worse than giving slow poison to the political opponents of the prime minister. This is more heinous than the incidents that occurred in Gujarat as a reaction to some incidents.

Therefore, *Mr. Alok Varma* did not obey the illegal orders from the PMO. In fact, no public servants shall obey the illegal orders of anyone.

Fearing an FIR against the PMO and the Prime Minister of India, the committee sacked him within 48 hours of reinstatement.

The Chief Justice of India could have taken this problem as a public interest litigation (PIL) stayed the decision of the committee, heard all sides and issued orders to *Mr. Alok Varma* to proceed against the PMO. He can do it even now.

But, it is shocking to note that the Chief Justice of India protects the PMO.

If a citizen of India goes through this work, he would agree that the present man fairly and adequately represents the1300 million people. He would tell that the court keeps him as an animal.

The present Chief Justice of India has not disposed of 38 well-meant letters submitted to him. He has done as much harm to the Indian judiciary as possible.

There is a conflict of interest also because of the following reasons. 1. The Supreme Court of India does violence against Article 39 of the Constitution of India 2. It, in very bad faith, deprives 1300 million people of their democratic political rights and 3. It refuses to recognize the fact that the present citizen fairly and adequately represents 1300 million absent class citizens.

The Chief Justice of India can use his residual powers to circulate the letters among the judges of the Supreme Court of India for their disposal.

If any judge of the Supreme Court of India thinks that he is free from the first two charges, he can take a decision on the third point and grant freedom to Indians consistent with the Constitution of India.

All other judges are accused persons liable for prosecution for bad faith actions. They cannot do justice to the 684 letters due to conflict of interests.

The present Parliament can continue until May 2019. If the elections get delayed, the present man must be sworn in as the Prime Minister of India after May 2019. The reason is that the present man fairly and adequately represents the 1300 million people.

# 39

# A question of interpretation

The Prime Minister of India, *Mr. Narendra Modi*, on 12 January 2019, addressed a BJP public meeting. He said, *"The Congress Government gave loans to fraudsters. Re.34 lakh core was given in the last six years of Congress governance and the total amount disbursed in the preceding 60 years was Re.18 lakh crore.*

*India suffered under Congress rule. Dynasty politics delayed progress in India. Congress lawyers are protecting the middlemen. India was unsafe before he assumed power. Opposite ideologies are now in alliance.*

*The BJP Government is a corruption-free government. There is not even a small corruption charge against the Government. We proved that the Government could be run without corruption. We must take Vajpayee's work forward. We are bringing back money to India.*

*The BJP treats each citizen equally. It is committed to farmer's welfare. We will double farmers income by 2022. We won't favor loan waiver short cut. Our efforts would be helpful in the long run.*

*Our Government worked with honesty in the last five years.*

*We don't claim everything is accomplished. We made sure tax income is spent in the right way. Only BJP promises a strong and stable Government. We want strong government to end loot.*

*Congress blocks justice. Congress disrespects national institutions. As the Chief Minister of Gujarat, I always faced Congress's torture. Congress tried everything to put as behind bars. But I always believed in our judiciary. We have complete faith in our judiciary"*

He talks like this because of the non -information of this work to the people.

The gas subsidy policy and the *Rafale offset clause* policy are against the essence of the Constitution of India. Yet, he claims that his government is free from corruption.

When a citizen of India points out things that are legal and constitutional, the Chief Justice of India must obey them. But he ignores. In contrast, when the Prime Minister of India says things that are illegal and unconstitutional, he obeys.

Former Central Bureau of Investigation (CBI) Director *Mr. Alok Varma* told the Chief Justice of India, in writing, that an official from the Prime Minister's Office (PMO) asked him to pursue the cases against *Mr. Lalu Prasad Yadav.* He added that he would disclose the name of the official provided the Chief Justice of India takes necessary action.

*Mr. Alok Varma* has the adequate standing to tell this to the Chief Justice of India. In fact, no other person in India is competent to tell this.

Above all, the entire world noticed it.

What should the Chief Justice of India do? He should have immediately asked him to file an affidavit or asked any other agency to file an FIR (First Information Report).

Any advocate anywhere in the India would give the above reply.

But he takes time to think over it. He would gather the support of other judges and come with a remedy after four or five days. This is to drag the other judges also into the pit.

He would tell the judges through his signs or words like this. 'See the Prime Minister of India cannot now directly talk to me. A few days ago, he said that we were obstructing justice. Now he says that he has complete faith in the judiciary. He says that it is his belief. We must understand the meaning of his words'.

The source of the authority of the Chief Justice of India is the Constitution of India. If he undermines the Constitution of India, his authority also would be undermined.

If the people think that the Chief Justice of India, warps or otherwise sufficiently mutilates the intent of the Constitution of India, **the authority of the Chief Justice of India would become a question of interpretation.**

# 40

# An apology

Defense Minister *Mrs. Nirmala Sitharaman,* on 12 January 2019, declared that the *Rafale* fighter jet would land in India very soon.

The *Rafale* case was not for determining the constitutionality or otherwise of the *Rafale agreement.* It was for a probe into some corruption charges.

It is customary for the Supreme Court of India to give its seal to the unconstitutional policy decisions after a shadow fight. The court knows that the petitioners need the seal of the Supreme Court of India to carry out the agreement. They, in fact, did not cite any section of the Constitution of India before the court.

About the corruption charges, the court held that *"the perception of individuals cannot be the basis of a fishing and roving enquiry'.* However, during the hearing, the bench asked the Government to file an affidavit on **the decision -making process.**

The affidavit clearly stated that the agreement was not placed before the Union Cabinet.

Thinking that the bench would overlook this, the present man said that 'the part cannot play the role of the whole' and wanted the court to declare it unconstitutional. Fearing more such points, the court covered up the letters and gave its green signal.

The offset clause vitiated Article 39 of the Constitution of India. The present man pointed out this point also. But the court decided to conceal the letters and gave a favorable verdict.

The people cannot function as judges of any court to adjudicate the cases or to do justice. But they can point out the Constitutional points to the judges so that they would not go astray. They do this for the integrity of the institution and for their progress.

If the Chief Justice had shown the letters to the people, he might not have done anything illegal.

At the instance of the ruling class, *Mr. Manohar Parrikar* had proposed the name of *Mr. Narendra Modi* for the post of the Prime Minister, in a BJP party convention. The ruling class gave great publicity to it and made him a prime minister. *Mr. Narendra Modi* made *Mr. Parrikar* the Defense Minister as a reciprocation.

The crucial point is *Mr. Parrikar* resigned and returned to the State level politics the moment he realized that *Mr. Narendra Modi* ignored his well-meant counsels while signing the agreement.

The present Defense Minister supports the *Rafale* agreement. The Defense Minister has become the instrument of the ruling class to extend its power. This is nothing but the show of strength of the ruling class. She forgets that the Constitution of India is legitimate only because of the consent of each person and any deal must be constitutional.

It must be reiterated that '**the sole and only function of the court shall be to decide if there was or was not a violation of an express provision or provisions of the Constitution and in the performance of**

**such functions the court must apply the Constitution to the cases before it'.**

But, notwithstanding several letters, the Supreme Court of India acted arbitrarily with the sole motive of extending the power of the ruling class in the defense deals.

*Retired Supreme Court of India judge Justice A.K. Patnaik,* on 12 January 2019, said that that there was no evidence of corruption against *Mr. Alok Varma.* He said that he supervised the Chief Vigilance Commission (CVC) probe. He added that the finding of the CVC does not belong to him.

It must be noted that he supervised the probe at the instance of Chief Justice of India *Ranjan Gogoi* only. He might have told him that he did not see any evidence of corruption against *Mr. Alok Varma.*

Yet, Chief Justice *Gogoi* did not unconditionally reinstate *Mr. Alok Varma.* He left his fate in the hand of the panel -the competent committee. This is because *Mr. Alok Varma* did not carry out the orders of the Prime Minister's Office (PMO) to pursue the cases against *Mr. Lalu Prasad Yadav.*

Prime Minister of India must have announced to the world that he had no special role in the *Mr. Lalu Prasad* case. He did not do so. Yet he attended the meeting and held that *Mr. Alok Varma* was guilty of dereliction of duty. This means that the direction of the PMO belonged to him.

*Mr. Alok Varma,* in writing, said that the PMO asked him to pursue the cases against *Mr. Lalu Prasad Yadav.* He expressed his readiness to disclose the name of the individual, if the Chief Justice of India is ready to act. But, latter did not allow *Mr. Alok Varma* to file even an FIR against the Prime Minister *Mr. Modi.*

The Prime Minister of India, *Mr. Narendra Modi*, should not have attended the panel meeting because of conflict of interests.  He wanted to keep a political in jail.  An accused cannot act against an important witness.

The Chief Justice of India also did not attend the meeting saying conflict of interests. But he should have informed the opinion of Justice Patnaik to the people. Then, the events might have taken the right course. But he did not do so. He should have at least conveyed the opinion of Justice Patnaik to *Justice A.K. Sikri.* Then the latter might have stoutly opposed the transfer of *Mr. Alok Varma.* He did not do. Thus, he slighted the opinion of *Justice Patnaik* on one side and trapped *Justice Sikri* on the other side.

The Chief Justice of India need not enter the cell *of Mr. Lalu Prasad Yadav* to keep him in jail. His actions have the effect of keeping him in jail. He is now an accused person. He has forfeited his right to constitute any bench remotely connected with *Mr. Alok Varma.*

Tomorrow, Justice *A.K. Sikri* would disown responsibility for the resolution of the panel. As a judge, he should not have joined a known accused to take a decision in his favor. He must tell the circumstances that led him to join the accused in the panel meeting.

A new judge - as per date of birth seniority, Justice. A.K.Sikri- must constitute the benches. There is nothing wrong in tendering **an apology** to the 1300 million people of India for not informing the contents of the 685 letters to them.

# 41

# The meaning of democracy

Prime Minister of India *Mr. Narendra Modi,* on 13 January 2019, said, "They want to build their own country"

A few days ago, he said, "They are day-dreaming to rule India".

His words give the impression that he is intercepting the emails.

The reason for the above conclusion is that the present man has not sent his last 40 letters to anyone other than the present Chief Justice of India.

The Supreme Court of India judge, *A.K. Sikri,* withdrew his consent to a government offer to nominate him for president/member in the London-based Commonwealth Secretariat Arbitral Tribunal (CSAT).

The media said that he gave his oral consent in December 2018. It kept it as a secret matter at that time. He withdrew the consent in writing on 13 January 2019. The media now reports it.

Three days ago, on 10 January 2019, he went with Prime Minister *Mr. Narendra Modi*, in recommending the transfer of *Central Bureau of Investigation (CBI) Director Mr. Alok Varma.*

After that, *Justice Patnaik* revealed that he did not notice any evidence of corruption against *Mr. Alok Varma* during his supervision.

In a letter, *Justice Sikri* told the Government that he was 'pained by the recent developments.

The developments would give pain to anyone.

As mentioned in the letter sent yesterday (13-1-2019), he rejected the offer because the Chief Justice of India *Ranjan Gogoi* did not convey the opinion of *Justice A.K. Patnaik* to him before attending the panel meeting led by the Prime Minister of India.

Alternatively, *Chief Justice Gogoi* might have asked him to side with the Prime Minister of India.

Anyhow, the decision to stand by the Prime Minister during the panel meeting was not his own thinking. The members of a committee often take this kind of stand when they are helpless or when they think that they could do nothing independently.

The letters from the present man might have prompted him to reject the offer from Prime Minister *Mr. Narendra Modi.*

However, what the present man knows is his letters and the present development. What happened in between is an imagination only.

Therefore, *Justice Sikri* must consider the question of revealing the facts that led him to support *Prime Minister Mr. Narendra Modi* in the panel meeting.

A new lawyer, *Mr. Shreya Singhal*, on 14 January 2019, challenged the decision of the Union Government to 'snoop: the data from any computer. The names of the petitioners were not disclosed. The names of the judges in the bench were also not known. It is customary for the media to report the names of the judges in the bench.

The Chief Justice of India is concealing essential facts and distorting the truth. It is an unfair judicial practice.

The Article 39 of the Constitution of India is not susceptible to two interpretations – one compatible and the other repugnant. If the implementation of this Article depends on the willingness of the Supreme Court of India or the Government of India, the Constitution of India would become meaningless. It is like subverting the Constitution of India.

**The Constitution of India demands democracy. Interpretation of this word must reflect the dictionary meaning of the word. The restrictive clauses are not for undoing it**. This is the standard interpretation followed all over the world.

The learned judges of the Supreme Court of India cannot be impeached for erroneous judgements or even for absurd judgements.

But they are subject to and bound by law.

The present man says that the present Chief Justice of India is an accused person. The Chief Justice must prove that he is not an accused

Now the Prime Minister of India and the Chief Justice of India are united in one thing – subversion of the Constitution of India.

The Chief Justice of India must come out of it for the benefit of 1300 million people and direct the competent authority to file an FIR for the charges levelled against Prime Minister *Mr. Narendra Modi* by former CBI Director *Mr. Alok Varma*. He had openly agreed to disclose the name of the official in the Prime Minister's Office (PMO) in support of his allegation. He placed one condition for that. The condition is that the Chief Justice of India must give an assurance to act.

The learned judges of the Supreme Court of India should have conducted rigorous analysis of the above problem and persuaded the Chief Justice of India to do his duty. The present man alone points out this. The learned judges of the Supreme Court of India must tell whether the Chief Justice of India must act immediately as demanded by the present man or not.

# 42

# The nature of the government

After releasing a book on former *Chief Justice of India Y.K. Sabharwal, Chief Justice of India Ranjan Gogoi,* on 14 January 2019, said that he wanted to be like ex-*Chief Justice of India Y.K Sabharwal.*

When *Mr. H.D. Deve Gowda* functioned as the Prime Minister of India, *Justice Y.K Sabharwal* was a judge of the Supreme Court of India. At the instance of the ruling class, *Justice Sabharwal* used the Supreme Court of India to pull down his government. The media mafia, Congress Party, Central Bureau of Investigation (CBI) and the other agencies played a complementary role.

At that time, he proclaimed to the world that all offenders are offenders and they should not be categorized. He used the CBI to chase the Congress leaders. This forced the then Congress President, *Mr.*

*Sitaram Kesri*, to withdraw the support of the Congress Party to the United Front (UF) Government led by *Mr. H.D. Deve Gowda*.

Then, he stood by the then *Prime Minister of India Mr. A.B. Vajpayee* to obliterate the Constitution of India in very bad faith. Despite 32 letters, he helped privatize 34 Public Sector Undertakings (PSUs) by doing violence to Articles 39 and 19 of the Constitution of India.

Present *Chief Justice of India Ranjan Gogoi* mars the chances of the present man to seize power and maintains status quo. *Justice Y.K. Sabharwal* pulled down a Government with consummate easy and made *Mr. A.B. Vajpayee* the Prime Minister of India twice.

Consistent with his service to the nation, his children are very rich.

No wonder, *Chief Justice of India Ranjan Gogo*i wants to be like former *Chief Justice of India Y.K. Sabharwal*. Even now he is like a super *Sabharwal*.

The vital point is that the judges and not the people make or mar the government.

*Chief Justice Ranjan Gogoi* can convert the present man into a prime minister or condemn him to death.

As in Maldives, the future of India is not in the hand of the people but in the hand of the Chief Justice of India.

About the CBI vote and the retirement offer of the Government of India, *Justice Sikri* said, "I expressed my unwillingness to attend the meeting. I told this to *Prime Minister Mr. Narendra Modi* and the Leader of the Opposition, *Mr. Mallikarjun Kharge*"

Further, he said, "I don't want the controversy to be dragged. Want it to die".

He is not ready to reveal what transpired between him and Chief Justice *Ranjan Gogoi*.

*Chief Justice Ranjan Gogoi* and *Justice A.K. Sikri* are one as for as *Mr. Lalu Prasad Yadav* and the 1300 million people of are concerned.

About *Mr. Lalu Prasad Yadav*, it must be stated that *Chief Justice of India Ranjan Gogoi* is the Accused No.1. He cannot morally and constitutionally function as the Chief Justice of India.

Even otherwise, he cannot function as the Chief Justice of India because he does violence to Articles 19 and 39.

Above all, he has not given a reply to 43 letters he received from the present citizen and the 645 letters received by his predecessors.

The present citizen deserves a reply.

If the submission of a citizen of India, makes it clear that he deserves a reply as to the Constitution of India, the Chief Justice of India can give a suitable reply. But he does not do so. He can give a reply only if he acts in good faith.

It can be easily seen, if most of the judges in the Supreme Court of India are proud of the actions of the Chief Justice of India *Ranjan Gogoi,* they would show *Mr. Narendra Modi* like leaders to the people. If they think that he is wrong in his ways, they would show the present man also to the people.

**The judges alone would determine the nature of the Government.**

# 43

# A farce

On 15 January 2019, Prime Minister of India *Mr. Narendra Modi* said. "There is a conspiracy to drive me out because my government had stopped the siphoning of Re.90,000 crore through bogus documents".

He says that he stopped the siphoning of Re. 90,000 crore. It confirms the worst fears of the people that money is being siphoned off continuously and that the Provident Fund and Pension Fund were siphoned off to unknown destinations with the connivance of the Supreme Court of India.

Why does he not inform the siphoning off money as and when it takes place?

He sees a conspiracy to drive him out. But he does not see a conspiracy to conceal this work from the eye of the people.

The Supreme Court of India can keep him in power until the conspiracy is unraveled.

A citizen of India says that the people would vote him to power, if the Supreme Court of India informs the contents of the 688 letters in its hand to them.

But the court is not ready to do the same.

*Mr. Narendra Modi* can continue as the Prime Minister of India without any election. Or the Supreme Court of India can ask *Mr. Rahul Gandhi* to take charge as the Prime Minister of India. There is no difference between their major policies although they talk differently. Both do violence to Article 19 and 39 to float as political leaders.

Why should India spend a huge amount of money to install any one of them or their nominee as the Prime Minister of India? Is it not a wastage of public money?

Why should the Supreme Court of India deceive the people and the entire world in the pretext of conducting an election?

There are reports that the Central Bureau of Investigation (CBI) tapped *National Security Adviser Ajit Doval's* phone. Apparently, former CBI Director *Mr. Alok Varma* had acknowledged it. Therefore, it is not a secret matter.

Prime Minister of India *Mr. Narendra Mo*di -led three-member committee had taken a decision to transfer CBI Director *Mr. Alok Varma* within three days of reinstatement. The committee relied on the report of former Supreme Court of India *Justice Patnaik*. But *Justice Patnaik* disowned the report. He said that his report did not mention any evidence of corruption by *Mr. Alok Varma*. The Leader of the Opposition, *Mr.Mallikarjun Kharge,* yesterday (15-1-2019) sought an answer from the Chief Justice of India. The media did not report it today.

How could this happen? The learned judges of the Supreme Court of India alone can give a reply, if they are proud of the. Chief Justice of India.

The learned judges of the Supreme Court of India continue to give very little weight to the Constitution of India. In fact, their silence over 688 letters raises doubts in the mind of the people. The provision in good faith cannot be utilized to overcome this specific problem.

The crucial issue is the non-information of this work to the people.

In 1995, the Supreme Court of India, through a judgement, said **that "every citizen has a fundamental right to impart as well as receive information".** This means that 1300 million people have a right to know the contents of the 688 letters.

In 2002, the Supreme Court of India said that **the non-information of works of this kind makes democracy** *a farce.*

This means that the Indian democracy is a farce according to the Supreme Court of India.

India is a democratic country as per the Constitution of India. Some say that democracy is the basic structure of the Constitution of India. They say democracy is the essence of the Constitution of India.

For democracy, the people must know this work. That does not happen. The judges must find a remedy for it.

**The learned judges of the Supreme Court of India have the power to use a given type of remedy if it is not expressly precluded in the Constitution of India. The only condition is that the remedy must be consistent with the essence of the Constitution of India.**

# 44

# Trilogy

Yesterday, on 16 January 2019, the *President of India, Mr. Ram Nath Kovind,* accepted the recommendation of the Supreme Court of India collegium to appoint *Justice Sanjiv Khanna* and *Denesh Maheshwari* as judges of the Supreme Court of India overlooking the seniority of *Chief Justices Pradeep Nandrajog* and *Rajendra Menon* the Chief Justices of the High Courts of Rajasthan and Delhi respectively.

Earlier, on 12 December 2018 the collegium comprising *Chief Justice of India Ranjan Gogoi* and *Justices Madan B. Lokur, A.K. Sikri, S.A. Bobde* and *N.B. Ramana* decided to recommend the names of *Justices Pradeep Nandrajog* and *Rajendra Menon* of the High Courts of Rajasthan and Delhi. After the retirement of *Justice Madan B. Lokur,* the new collegium discarded that decision.

According to some reports, *Justice Denesh Maheswari* superseded 32 judges.

It is customary to interpose a young judge to prevent the seniors becoming judges. The motive of the present elevation is not a clear one.

According to another report, *Supreme Court of India judge S. K. Kaul* requested the Chief Justice of India not to ignore the seniority of *Justices Pradeep Nandrajog* and *Rajendra Menon.*

It is not customary for the media to report the differences among the judges of the Supreme Court of India. Further, it is very strict now-a-days. It did not report the farewell function extended to *Justice Madan B. Lokur.* Yet, it reported the action taken by *Justice S.K. Kaul.* However, the Chief Justice of India administered the oath of office today (17-1-2019) to them.

Thus, a day passed like this.

It may be recalled that on 12 January 2018, four judges of the Supreme Court of India addressed a press conference. They alleged that democracy was not safe in the hand of then *Chief Justice of India Dipak Misra. Justice Rajan Gogoi* was one of them. It is now clear that *Chief Justice Ranjan Gogoi,* camouflaged as a lover of freedom penetrated the rank of three other judges with the objective known to him.

What is known today is that the successive chief justices of India together with the judges of the Supreme Court of India do violence against the Articles 19 and 39 of the Constitution of India. It is their politics.

A few judges might oppose it. But they cannot do anything. Even if they do something, it would end as a storm in the tea cup as the media would not report them.

As the judges have taken away the political rights of the people, the Indians have not seen democracy even for a day.

The judges of the Supreme Court of India have an interest in maintaining an illegitimate government. The politics of India is the politics of the judges. Their politics keeps *Mr. Narendra* as the prime minister. They can retain him if they want. Or they can invite *Mr. Rahul*

*Gandhi*. If they don't want both, they can project the present man. But, it may not be in the interest of the ruling class to show the present man. Thus, they decide the outcome of the elections in favor of the first two.

Elections are conducted only as a show. They are not necessary under the present conditions.

The Constitution of India demands the judges to be constitutional in their ways. Just as the people must remain under the Constitution of India, the judges also must remain under the Constitution of India.

A citizen of India may not do as much as this work in future to challenge the existing leaders. But his right is being abridged. **The amount suffered by each citizen may be small but the principle large.**

It is true that the judges cannot act like a "philosopher king'. A judge of the Supreme Court of India has no authority to develop a 'Solomon-like' solution and impose it upon the people as in the *Rafale* judgement. His authority is limited to deciding whether the grievances have constitutional merit or not.

The present man thinks that his demand has constitutional merit.

The present man says that the learned judges of the Supreme Court of India do violence against Articles 19 and 39 of the Constitution of India and maintain an illegitimate government.

**Therefore, the judges have power under the Trilogy to achieve justice even if they think that it is a situation not contemplated or covered by the Constitution of India.**

If most of the judges are not for it, one would think that they play treasonable politics to keep *Mr. Narendra Modi* or *Mr. Rahul Gandhi* in power.

If the Chief Justice of India does not circulate these letters, the judges would not know anything about them.

He is free to do anything.

# 45

# The capricious will

The media yesterday (17 January 2019), disclosed that the Chief Justice of India, *Ranjan Gogoi,* got some incriminating materials against the two High Court judges- *Pradeep Nandrajog* and *Rajendra Menon –* after the Supreme Court collegium on 12 December 2018 decided to elevate them as the judges of the Supreme Court of India.

He might have obtained similar incriminating materials against the 32 superseded judges of the High Courts. According to the present collegium, the High Courts are replete with criminals and these 32 judges cannot aspire to become judges of the Supreme Court of India.

The present man repeatedly said that the judges should not be selected arbitrarily. But in India, liberties and properties are not dependent on rules and laws but **the capricious will of the Chief Justice of India.**

During the impeachment trial of Warren Hastings in 1788, *Edmund Bruke* said, ***"Those who give and those who receive arbitrary power are alike criminal"***.

The present Chief Justice of India uses the arbitrary power nakedly. Therefore, according to *Edmund Bruke*, Chief Justice *Ranjan Gogoi* is the No.1 criminal in India. He converted 32 High Court judges into criminals in one stroke.

A judge of the Supreme Court of India, *Justice Kaul*, had – in writing- asked the Chief Justice of India not to supersede the 32 judges. His letter has the effect of a court order. The Chief Justice of India should not have administered the oath of office before disposing of his letter through a duly constituted bench.

If the 32 judges approach the High Courts for remedy, one would see conflict of interests. But, why did they not approach the Supreme Court of India? After all, the members of the collegium cannot hear the case due to conflict of interest.

If substantial number of judges refuse to seek relief against unjust actions of the collegium, what would happen to ordinary people?


Finance Minister of India *Mr. Arul Jaitely* yesterday said, *"Some people think that they are born to rule India."*

The present man said that the people might have chosen him as the Prime Minister of India if the Supreme Court of India had shown the first thirty-two letters to the people. This means *Dr. Manmohan Singh* and *Mr. Narendra Modi* might not have become prime ministers.

Even now, the people would choose the present man as their leader if the present Chief Justice of India is ready to show the 45 letters received by him. No doubt that the Indians sacrificed their future by choosing *Dr. Manmohan Singh* and *Mr. Narendra Modi*.

India needs strong leadership. How will the people measure the strength of a leader? A leader must be strong enough to face an election in an atmosphere of freedom.

*Mr. Narendra Modi* could not have fought the last election in an atmosphere of freedom. But he got five years to enlarge the freedom of Indians. But he could not make the letters available to the people.

The instinct of any prime minister would be to rule India by denying freedom of expression. But he should have defied the Supreme Court of India in this matter and declared freedom to Indians as soon as assuming office. Then, he could have told the Indians: 'See, I have granted freedom to you to know men and matters according to degree. Even Gandhiji, Nehru, Vallabhbhai Patel or their successors did not dare to give it'. .

But he could not acquire the necessary courage to deliver freedom. He continues as a poor tea maker. He runs for cover for every letter. This shows that he is not a strong leader. This alone is sufficient to disqualify him.

But he wants to join the Chief Justice of India to rig the elections. What will his supporters think about him if they get a chance to see the letters?

It is true that the judges of the Supreme Court of India cannot defy the Chief Justice of India and constitute benches. But, they can take the matter to the people. The media would not allow the people to know this good fortune, but the chances of success are very great.

The crucial question is whether the judges could violate Article 19 and 39 and rig the elections to project *Mr. Narendra Modi* as the leader of the people?

**The judges would be remiss in their responsibilities as judges of the Supreme Court of India, if they refuse to give their ruling to the above question particularly when a citizen of India needs such a ruling.**

The ruling that they make may not be self-enforcing. But the public opinion would force the Chief Justice of India to abide by their ruling.

Assume that the present man tries to magnify the importance of the letters. Then, his complaints might shrink in importance and it might enable the judges to dispose of the letters easily.

The Constitution of India allows the judges to give their ruling based on the merits of the grievance placed before them by the people as and when their liberties are threatened by the Chief Justice of India.

Every judge of the Supreme Court of India must receive, hear and consider seriously and sympathetically the grievance of the citizens. They must try to make it an occasion for additional education of the people and to remove the wrinkles from their faces.

The Chief Justice of India is requested to use his residual powers to circulate this letter among all judges of the Supreme Court of India. Any refusal would be breach of trust. The judges shall share the letters with outsiders only with the knowledge of the people of India ie only if the media publishes the letter.

# 46

# Rooted in the Constitution

To justify the supersession of 32 High Court judges the media on 19 January 2019, said that the collegium had rescinded its decisions on nine occasions in the last 10 years.

The collegium operates under a general policy of discrimination against the individuals capable of upholding the rule of law. Its decisions are not based on merits or any promulgated rules. Therefore, until the judges prove otherwise, the people cannot trust the judges selected by the collegium.

The 32 affected judges should have filed a writ petition before a bench headed by a judge of the Supreme Court of India.

They cannot approach the bench headed by the Chief Justice of India due to conflict of interests.

Therefore, they must approach the other judges for relief.

*Mr. Bill Gates,* on 18 January 2019, congratulated Prime Minister of India *Mr. Narendra Modi* for his health insurance scheme.

The States like Tamil Nadu had been implementing this scheme. So, it is not *Mr. Modi's* scheme. Further, *Mr. Modi* would hand over the scheme to his promoters only. They are going to mint money like anything.

Many big people all over the world commend Prime Minister *Mr. Modi.* TV channels show that the people love him lavishly and extravagantly. He says that he made India a fastest growing economy. Above all, he says that there are no people apart from him in India. Why should India conduct an election and spend a huge amount of money? He can continue as the Prime Minister of India and go ahead like this.

The Prime Minister of India, *Mr. Narendra Modi,* on 19 January 2019, said that some people were going to attribute his victory to the Electronic Voting Machine (EVM).

The act of manipulating the EVMs is a smaller crime than the act of depriving the people of their political rights. He can very well do both simultaneously with consummate easy. The people would not know anything.

It must be noted that the Election Commission of India (ECI) has not given the reason for substituting the ballot paper by the EVMs.

The Election Commission of India (ECI) on 18 January 2019, disclosed that the elections would be announced in the first week of March 2019.

There exists a conspiracy to rig the elections by concealing the letters of the present man from the people.  The Chief Justice of India, *Ranjan Gogoi,* is the **epicenter of the conspiracy**.

The grievances are problems to be solved and not arguments to be proved.

A citizen of India says that the Supreme Court of India takes away the political rights of 1300 million people to know men and matters according to degree. The court thus violates Article 19.

As the people should not be allowed to know this, the media all over the world is not ready to inform this work to the people. Therefore, all attempts of the present man to reach the people failed.

As the present man has the standing to say this, the Supreme Court of India should have taken appropriate measures to convey the views of the present man to the people.

But, contrary to the express language of the Constitution of India, the Supreme Court of India refuses to give a reply to 691 letters. It has proved that it exists as an institution only to- take away the democratic rights of the people. It simply projects *Mr. Narendra Modi* as a potential candidate.

An ordinary man cannot approach the Supreme Court of India with a writ petition. Even if someone approaches it with one, the media would not report it to the people

Therefore, a citizen of India approaches the learned judges of the Supreme Court of India for their interpretation. The Constitution of India does not impose any limitation upon the judges to give the democratic rights to the people. Their interpretation must be based on the Constitution of India.

Their interpretation may conflict with the convention. **The only condition is that it must be 'rooted' in the Constitution of India.** Their interpretation of the nature of the issue is entitled to the same deference as their other routine judgements and the Chief Justice of India cannot substitute his interpretation.

# 47

# Right to life

The media today (21-1-2019) said that the Government of India had paid Re. 35000 crore for the *Rafale* fighter jet.

The *Refale* case was for a probe into some acts of corruption. It was not to determine the constitutionality or otherwise of the offset clause of the *Rafale* agreement.

Further, no erroneous judgement shall be enforced by the court. The code of professional responsibility demands this.

The offset clause violates the plain language of the Article 39 of the Constitution of India. It was duly informed to the Supreme Court of India.

It is not feasible for a citizen of India to file a writ petition in the Supreme Court of India. The Chief Justice of India should have – at least- informed the points presented by the present man to the people. He did not do so. His duty is to prevent exploitation. But he exploits the ignorance of the people. Therefore, he is the Accused No.1 in the *Rafale* case.

It must be noted that it is not for his judgement but for misusing his position through bad-faith actions.

As the Chief Justice of India sits in a safe place, his actions manifest disregard of the Constitution of India.

A citizen of India - after making incalculable contribution to nation building - says that the Chief Justice of India takes away the political rights of 1300 million people in violation of Article 19. It is the finding of a citizen. It is not a wonder that a citizen – after 18 years of continuous work- discerns the problem in new highlight. He seeks a peaceful, prompt and just solution from the Chief Justice of India. The latter must understand the problem, constitute a bench and give a sound judgement within a specified time. If he sees a conflict, he can ask the other judges to give their judgement.

The Supreme Court of India occasionally says that Article 21 can be claimed when a citizen is deprived of his life or personal liberty by the state as defined in Article 19. Article 21 prohibits the deprivation of the above rights. The right to life is not merely a physical right. **The court says that the right to life includes the right to life with human dignity and all those aspects of life which goes to make man's life meaningful, complete and worth living.**

But, the Chief Justice of India remains motionless. Under these conditions, the other judges of the court should not leave the matter to the judgement of the out-siders, but they must sit in a bench to find a solution.

# 48

# Uncivilized methods

A *Mr.Syed Shuja* - in a press meet - disclosed that the 2014 general elections to Indian Parliament was rigged by hacking the Electronic Voting Machines (EVMs). He added that the elections to Bihar, Utter Pradesh and Delhi states were also rigged by tampering the EVMs.

He claimed that he was a former employee of the Electronic Corporation of India and was a part of the team that tested whether the machines could be hacked or not. The team found a way to hack into the machine but then all members of the team except him were killed in a shootout. He claimed that he was also shot but somehow survived and managed to reach the USA.

The time of shootout, place of shootout and the total number of employees killed by the shootout were not revealed. But Congress Leader *Kapil Sibal* was present during the above press meet. The court could know the rest from him.

The New Indian Express reported the above press meet today (22-1-2019).

The tendency of the people would be to reject the revelation as a figment of imagination. But it must be a fact.

The reason for the conclusion is that the Supreme Court of India takes away the political rights of the people. Now, it is concealing even the leader of the opposition in the Parliament. It projects Prime Minister *Mr. Narendra Modi* alone.

A court that exists to take away the political rights of the people, would manipulate the EVMs without the slightest compunction. It is very easy.

It knew that it can do any crime with the support of the media mafia.

Prime Minister of India *Mr. Narendra Modi* does not appear like a true political leader because he – just like the Supreme Court of India- takes away the political rights of the people.

Further, the Election Commission of India (ECI) has not given the reason for introducing the EVMs although the Constitution of India says that the elections should be by ballot.

The Constitution of India is an agreement for making all Indians equal with respect to political rights. The people agreed to surrender all their rights for unilateral action like agitations and others thinking that a show of economic strength would not mar the objectivity of the judges.

Thus, the people were made to assume that the Supreme Court of India would protect their rights.

The founding fathers of the Constitution of India assured that the judges of the Supreme Court of India would look at the grievances of the people objectively and a reasonable decision based upon the true merits of the grievances could be expected.

But the learned judges of the Supreme Court of India remain motionless for 695 letters from a citizen of India. They would even listen to their household servants and advocates but not to the present citizen of India. No one would believe this!

**However, they must prove that the people could find a solution to their grievances through judicial methods rather than thorough any other uncivilized methods.**

# 49

# Dismembering the Constitution

The Chennai bench of the Madras High Court, on 23 January 2019, directed the striking employees of the Government of Tamil Nadu to join duty on or before January 25, 2019. The case is being heard by the Madurai bench of the Madras High Court also.

The doctrine of non-interference or the doctrine of judicial stability demands that the courts of equal and co-ordinate jurisdiction cannot interfere with each other's jurisdiction. This principle also bars a court from reviewing or interfering with the judgement or proceeding of a co-equal court over which it has no appellate jurisdiction.

Why did the Chennai bench interfere with the proceedings of the Madurai bench? Are the judges not aware of the Principles in remedial law?

Whatever happened, the motive of the Chennai bench is to do more harm to the striking employees than the Madurai bench.

Defense Minister *Mrs. Nirmala Sitharaman*, on 23 January 2019, said that the Supreme Court of India had not found anything wrong with the offset clause of the *Rafale agreement*.

The case filed by advocate *Mr. Prasant Bhusan* and others in the *Rafale* matter was for a probe. It did not ask the court to declare the *Rafale agreement* an *unconstitutional one*.

*The Rafale agreement* vitiates Articles 39 and 19 and, therefore, unconstitutional.

Further, after getting a favorable judgement, the Government wanted to correct it. The petitioners wanted to recall it. The present citizen said. that the court cannot, correct, delete, add or recall it. The court accepted the view of the present man and so, remained quiet after secretly informing it to the parties.

The *Rafale judgement* does not totally deprive the court of its jurisdiction over the judgement. What the court lost is the power to amend, modify, add, delete or alter the judgement.

The judges of the Supreme Court of India must strive to give effect to the Constitution of India rather than to dismember it.

When more than one interpretation are possible, the one closer to the Constitution of India must be taken.

As the view of the present man is closer to the Constitution of India, the court should have accepted it.

Further, when there is a conflict between Articles 39 and the judgement, Article 39 would prevail. When a judgement violates Article 19, Article 19 would prevail.

As the court did not reckon this, the *Rafale judgement* **dismembers the Constitution of India.**

Therefore, under no circumstances the erroneous judgements shall be enforced.

The Union Government or the court shall not deceive the people in the pretext of a wrong or erroneous judgement.

The Supreme Court of India must direct the Government to tell the reason why it enforced the *Rafale agreement* citing the Supreme Court of India judgement.

There are reports that the outcome of the 2014 elections to the Indian Parliament was determined by the Reliance Industries Limited (RIL) by remotely manipulating the signals of the Electronic Voting Machines (EVM). Further, *Congress Leader Mr. Kapil Sibal* wanted an enquiry into the allegations of the former employee of the Electronic Corporation of India, *Mr. Shuja.*

The elections are being rigged. The act of manipulating the signals is a small offence compared to the act of depriving the people of their right to know men and matters.

Further, as the RIL allegedly manipulated the elections, the Supreme Court of India would say that the RIL earned the right to do it because of its wealth.

Even when the elections were by ballot, some constituencies registered nil invalid votes in one of the general elections. There were some other anomalies like this. The people used to wonder at some results because the crowd support did not tally with the results.

Therefore, the ballot paper system cannot be free from one kind of manipulation or other. But, it cannot be the reason for substituting it by the EVM system

If the Prime Minister of India is impartial in his official duties, the TV channels would show the real crowd support for different leaders and the people would be in a better position to gauge the outcome. Now the TV channels carefully avoid showing the crowd support for the leaders.

It is great that *Mr. Kapil Sibal* attended the press meet of *Mr. Shuja.*

*Mr. Sibal* was a Union Cabinet Minister in the UPA Government. He was one of very few leaders behind the impeachment motion against *former Chief Justice of India Dipak Misra.* He is a renowned advocate of the Supreme Court of India. The fact that he attended the press meet reinforced its importance.

Perhaps, India escapes from the fangs and claws of the Supreme Court of India only because of such people.

However, he, in his capacity as a Cabinet Minister, signed the papers that allowed the Election Commission of India (ECI) to have radio waves in the EVMs. As he is not aware of the reasons, he could have asked the officials – through the Supreme Court of India or directly - to tell the purpose of radio waves in the EVMs.

Whatever happened, the people are poised to ditch *Prime Minister of India Mr. Narendra Modi* for his show unless he comes with some miracles in the impending budget. But Congress Party is a greater threat to the loved liberties of the people because it refused to grant freedom to the people for 10 years.

The crucial question is whether the manipulation of the EVMs occurred with the knowledge of *Mr. Mukesh Ambani* or not. The allegation could be true or false. But the cogent happenings must be analyzed.

If the RIL manipulated the machines during the UPA rule, there is no reason for the BJP to defend the ECI. But the BJP wants EVMs and the UPA wants the ballot paper.

This gives the impression that the EVMs were indeed manipulated to the advantage of the BJP.

Further, the BJP Government under *Prime Minister of India Mr. Modi* gave away Re.59000 crore in the pretext of gas subsidy. *'We gave the subsidy to the people. The people, in turn, used their discretion to transmit it to the RIL. What can we do? We did not give anything directly to the RIL. We don't loot the nation. We have the seal of the Supreme Court of India. Our hands are free'* This is the stand of *Prime Minister Mr. Modi.* Had the RIL not manipulated the EVMs, *Mr. Modi* might not have obliged to give the money to it.

Similarly, *Prime Minister of India Mr. Modi* said, *"We gave the money to a French company. That company wants to transmit the money to Mr. Anil Ambani. We don't give the money to Mr. Anil Ambani. The French company uses its discretion to give the money to Mr. Anil Ambani. What can we do? We have the seal of the Supreme Court of India. Our hands are free."* Anyone can discern that the offset clause of the *Rafale agreement* is directly related to the EVM manipulation.

There was allegation of a shootout resulting in the death of 11 engineers. But, the media talks of the death of three persons in some other place. If the shootout had not occurred, the media might have capitalized on it to rebut the allegation. Now the media is silent about the shootout. The intelligence agencies also do not accept or deny the allegation.

True or false, everyone needs the answer of the Supreme Court of India.

Everything shows that if the Supreme Court of India rots, all other institutions, Government of India, State Governments, intelligence agencies and the media would rot.

The Supreme Court of India ignores or pretend to ignore this matter. It should have treated the revelation as a writ petition and taken the matter to its logical conclusion because the media, CBI, RAW and other agencies must be aware of it. It has not done so.

Further, the learned judges of the Supreme Court of India are expected to be impartial in their judgements. But, they show extraordinary interest in projecting the BJP and the Congress Party through the media and conceal this work. It projects even *Mrs. Priyanka Gandhi* with immense importance. In this way, they take away the political rights of the people. "He is like an ant. Why should we project him? By taking this stand, they take away the democratic rights of the people.

Thus, the people try to find out the cause from the effects. Can the court deny it?

The Chief Justice of India cannot accept the letters as a writ petition or do justice in any other way due to conflict of interests

Therefore, this letter is being submitted to *Justice Indira Banerjee* of the Supreme Court of India in the hope that she would gather the support of other judges to do justice to 695 letters and to give political rights to 1300 million people.

# 50

# The Holmesian Adage

After several letters, the Chief Election Commissioner (CEC) of India, *Mr. Sunil Arora*, yesterday (24 January 2019), gave the reason for substituting the ballot paper by the Electronic Voting Machines (EVM). The reasons were: 1. Booth capturing 2. Impersonation and 3. Inordinate delay in declaring results.

Anyone would tell that these are trivial reasons. Impersonation can be controlled due to Aadhar (Unique Identification Number). Booth capturing occurs even with the EVMs. A few hours delay would not change the outcome. Even if some unwanted things occur, everyone could tell with certainty what happened and appropriate remedial measures could be taken.

In contrast, with the EVMs, none can say anything except expressing doubt in the process. Therefore, it is the duty of the ECI to dispel this doubt from the mind of the people.

He said that Election Commission of India (ECI) would not be coerced into using ballot papers. In this matter, the Constitution of India demands election by ballot paper. It is his duty to obey the Constitution of India and not the present man. He has no prerogative to change the system of election.

*Mr. Arora* did not reveal the purpose of radio waves in the EVMs. He did not tell anything about the shootout that resulted in the death of 11 engineers. He did not give any satisfactory reply to the allegation of *Mr. Syed Shuja.*

Above all, he did not tell anything about enforcing freedom of expression.

The present man submitted 695 letters to the Supreme Court of India since June 2001. The first 645 letters were sent to the President of India. Different letters were sent to the Prime Minister of India, Election Commission of India (ECI), Central Bureau of Investigations (CBI), National Human Rights Commission (NHRC), Chief Vigilance Commissioner (CVC), Members of Parliament, Chief Ministers, Chief Justices of High Courts, Members of State Assemblies, United Nations (UN), newspapers and the TV channels all over the world, blogs and the YouTube. But none tells anything about the letters to the illiterate people of India. This has the effect of depriving the people of their political rights. **The old Holmesian adage that the best test of truth is in the open market is applicable to the present condition in India.** But, the people have no way to choose their representatives.

The ECI would say that the individual damages are comparatively small because the illiterate people are not conscious of their democratic rights. But he must note that the aggregate damage is very great. Now, action should not be denied simply because the damage is a frightening one. The unlawful conduct of the ECI, in fact, pre-empted the chances of the present man to become the Prime Minister of India on three occasions.

If the people had seen this work, all public resources might have been restored and several other things consistent with the Constitution of India might have occurred. This might have made the present man the natural choice of the people.

Now the ECI  has no prerogative to conduct the general elections after abridging the rights of the people to vote. **It is not the physical ability of a person to vote. It is his mental ability to vote.** Therefore, reasonable chance must be given to the people to know news and views before the election.

The ECI would come to know about this letter only if the Supreme Court of India directs the media to publish it. Therefore, unless otherwise prevented, he would rig the elections as usual.

The high-level selection committee comprising the Prime Minister of India, the leader of the opposition and the Chief Justice of India met yesterday to select a new Director for the CBI. The meeting was inconclusive. It would meet again next week.

It must be noted that the former Director, *Mr. Alok Varma*, was ousted from the CBI quite unconstitutionally. The reason is that the disciplinary authority and the appellate authority cannot be the same. *Mr. Alok Varma* cannot appeal to the Supreme Court of India. Even if he appeals, the Supreme Court of India cannot hear his case due to conflict of interests. These are the basic things in law. This happened in the *Justice Karnan* case. As the people have no chance to see the letters, it repeats.

In the *Alok Varma case,* the Supreme Court of India, as in many other instances, dismembered the Constitution of India in very bad faith. Therefore, he must be reinstated forthwith and allowed to function for two years consistent with the contract between the court and the Government.

Further, all actions of the Supreme Court of India are null and void if it denies freedom to the people. **'No doubt, a judge or a bench will take greater care to make the judgement clear and the reasoning logical if it is known that the judgement will be subject to public inspection'**. Otherwise, any bench would deliver any unconstitutional judgements in very bad faith.

Thus, the publication of these letters is an effective way to help ensure accountability of judges.

The welfare of the country also demands that the expressions of experience of the present citizen be made available to the people.

As the Chief Justice of India cannot dispose of the letters, this letter is being submitted to *Justice R. Banumathi* in the profound hope that she would release it to the media. The last letter was sent to *Justice Indira Banerjee.*

# 51

# The people must present reasons rather than arms.

The Chennai bench of the Madras High Court diluted its stand over the striking employees yesterday (25 January 2019). It said, "We did not stay the strike. It is for the Government to take action". The changed stand may be due to the letter sent to *Justice Indira Banerjee* of the Supreme Court of India day-before- yesterday.

But what the present man knows is his letter and the present stand of the High Court. What happened in between is an imagination only.

India today conferred *Bharat Reta,* the highest civilian award to former President of India, *Mr. Pranab Mukherjee.*

It may be recalled that the NDA Government had privatized 34 Public Sector Undertakings (PSUs). After that, the UPA Government came to power. He was a powerful minister in it. He knew the language of the Constitution of India. The choice before him was clear: **either class action or no action.** He chose the latter one.

One day, the Supreme Court of India cancelled the petrol outlets sanctioned by the Members of Parliament (MPs) in the pretext of corruption and favoritism on the part of the MPs. Next day, it permitted the Reliance Industries Limited (RIL) to distribute the same all over India. *Mr. Pranab Mukherjee* did not deem it his duty even to put right this.

**Societies want to increase public power over the natural resources.** Article 39 of the Constitution of India specifically demands this because it comes under the Directive Principles. The people fought for independence mainly for this. The plain and unambiguous words of Article 39 are undisputed facts. But he helped alienate the natural resources like coal, iron to private parties.

He played an active role in the privatization of Mumbai and Delhi airports.

He sent Re.3 lakh crore in the Provident Fund and another Re. 3 lakh crore in the Pension Fund to unknown destinations.

As the President of India, he projected *Prime Minister Mr. Narendra Modi* and *Congress leader Mr. Rahul Gandhi* as national leaders and suppressed the contributions of the present man. It is true that his predecessors could not make the media to publish the letters received from the present man. **But the established practice should not be used to set aside the Constitution of India.**

Similarly, a past practice many be an exception to the widespread application of a written constitution. As the language of the Constitution of India is plain and un-ambiguous, he should not have relied on the past practices but given democracy to Indians before the 2014 General Elections. But he imparted great legitimacy to *Prime Minister Mr. Modi* and *Congress leader Mr. Rahul Gandhi.* The people simply thought that there were no people apart from them in India. Thus, he kept the people like animals.

**It is a mark of civilization that people present reasons rather than arms.** Boland said it.

After the 2014 election also, he received hundreds of letters from the present citizen of India. The people should have known the salient points of these letters as a natural consequence of his presidency. But, it did not happen. Thus, he abridged the freedom of the people to know men and matters until his last day last minute in office. It went down as a crime against humanity.

These are all described in the book titled **'The Pranab Effects'**.

Yet, he has been awarded the Bharat Retna. The present man would say that he got it in recognition of his ability to take away the political rights of the people.

Notwithstanding everything, if former Prime Minister *Mr.A.B. Vajpayee* could be given Bharath Retna, he too deserves it. *Mr. Narendra Modi, Mr. Arun Jaitely, Jaswant Sinha, Mr. P. Chithambaram, Dr. Manmohan Singh* and many other past and present Union Ministers would come in the same series.

The President of India, *Mr. Ram Nath Kovind,* in his Republic Day message on 25 January 2019, requested the people to see the 2019 General Election as the "one-in-a-century moment. How can a general election that comes at least once in every five years for rotating the prime minister-ship be "one-in-a-century" moment? Does he intend to give freedom to Indians?

It must be stated that the President of India has no prerogative to conduct an election after abridging the freedom of the people. Anyhow, the people are waiting for that 'moment'.

There was a time when there were no female judges in the Supreme Court of India. At that time, the present man told the Chief Justice of India that there must be 50 percent reservation for the females in the judiciary. The reason is that the women are remarkable in their power of judgement.

The present man believes that women, as a rule, take immense pride in their acts of redress of public wrongs. Further, Indian women live for others – for their own children, family and the people at large.

Therefore, this letter is being submitted to *Justice Indu Malhotra,* the third and the last female judge of the Supreme Court of India.

She is requested to release this letter to the media for the lasting welfare of the people. She could think of other actions only if the media refuses to publish it.

No doubt, it is *an exception* to the general practice. As the Chief Justice of India cannot dispose of the letters due to conflict of interests, the  present man approaches other judges to fulfil the needs of the people.

It is true that it is not customary for other judges to obey the people. Here, the judge obeys the Constitution of India and not the present man. It is the prerogative of the judge to adjudicate any petition, if the Chief Justice of India cannot act on it. **'Mere non- use of a right does not entail a loss of it.'**

The information of this letter to the people would not belittle the judiciary because **'if a judgement is worthy, it would survive open market inspection'.**

# 52

# It is not the prerogative of the court

The Government of Tamil Nadu described the restoration of the old pension system to its employees as an impossibility due to the very poor financial conditions. According to some reports, the Chief Minister of Tamil Nadu refused to invite the striking employees for talks.

There was a strike in the Kerala State when *Mr. A.K. Antony* was functioning as the Chief Minister of Kerala. It lasted for more than a month. *Chief Minister Mr. Antony* refused to invite the leaders for talks. The public stood by him. The employees lost all hopes. The present man, then requested the Chief Minister to invite the leaders for talks and concede their demands with the condition that they would get the monetary benefits as and when the financial condition improves. In the same letter, he was requested to grant permission to start 10 medical colleges and 100 Engineering Colleges under the self-financing policy.

Within 24 hours of the receipt of the letter, the Chief Minister accepted all demands of the employees even without calling them for talks. The self - financing colleges also were introduced for the first time in Kerala. He acknowledged the receipt of the letter with his own signature.

Similarly, in June 2003, the Government of Tamil Nadu dismissed more than 2 lakh striking employees. Unemployed hands were recruited on a war footing. The public said that the dismissed employees would loiter in the streets. The employees were shocked by the action of the Government. More than 20 died of heart attack.

The present man sent his letter No.20 on July 2003 to the President of India and the Chief Justice of India. In that letter, the present man said that the state must be an ethical institution.

A judge in the Madras High Court was twisting the case to the disadvantage of the employees like anything. Whatever happened, within 24 hours, the judge asked the petitioners to give the arguments as a written statement, reserved the judgement and reached Madurai by car.

At that time, the present man had not much standing. Therefore, the President of India and the Chief Justice of India could have ignored the letter. But they did not do so.

The present man felt that they acted as swiftly as possible.

The Government of Tamil Nadu could not understand anything. Four ministers flew to Delhi and returned empty handed. On 10 July 2003, all were reinstated by the court. These are mentioned in the book "Prime Minister A.B. Vajpayee and the Abdication of Power".

Now, the Chief Minister of Tamil Nadu can invite the employees for talks and restore the old pension scheme. The financial burden to his Government will be a negligible one because the employee would retire after many years. He need not think about the burden of the future governments.

If he comes to power, he can demand a share in the Hindustan Zinc Limited (HZL). Its profit per year is Re. 1,00,000 crore. Where does this money go? It goes into the hand of someone known to the present Prime Minister of India. The income from other privatized Public-Sector Undertakings is not reckoned.

There was Re.3,00,000 crore in the Provident Fund and another Re.3,00,000 crore in the Pension Fund when the UPA came to power. Where did this money go? No chief minister knows this because it went in the hand of someone known to the present judges of the Supreme Court of India. He can approach them for a reasonable share.

The Supreme Court of India and President of India must see that the *Miss. Anitha* and the 2003 episodes do not repeat in this matter. The present man sent a letter to the President of India 48 hours before the death of *Miss. Anitha.* If he had acted promptly, the media might have reported the letter to the people,  and she might not have committed suicide.

Now, if the Supreme Court of India cannot direct the media to publish this letter, it can ask the Chief Minister of Tamil Nadu to do the needful to prevent the repeat of *Miss. Anitha and the 2003 episodes.*

Incidentally, *Prime Minister of India Mr. Narendra Modi* can restore the Old Penson Scheme in the impending budget only to defeat the dynasty politics.


*The New Indian Express* today said that the Government has five major responsibilities. They are law and order, defense, transport, education and health care.

According to the paper, the people must get food and water like animals and that they need not know news and views. Therefore, it did not mention freedom under the five major responsibilities.

The Prime Minister of India, *Mr. Narendra Modi*, today (27 January 2019, said, *"Any person who has cheated the nation will be punished"*

His gas subsidy scheme and the offset clause of the *Rafale agreement* dismember the Constitution of India. They might not come under cheating. He might have treated them as treasonable offences. Therefore, he says that others cheated the nation.

Further, he said. "We must understand that casting vote is our responsibility"

He must give political rights to the people to know news and views. Now, he does not show anyone other than him and sparingly *Mr. Rahul Gandhi*. The people have lost their thinking faculty because they don't see anyone other than the people shown by him.

It must be stated that the Supreme Court of India noticed clear and **convincing evidence of wrongdoing by the media**. It is its duty to issue orders in the form of mandatory injunctions that command the media to take some affirmative action.

For the above, the learned judges of the Supreme Court of India need not be experts in constitutional matters. They must know **that it is not the prerogative of the Supreme Court of India to conduct elections after denying the political rights of the people.**

To make its intentions clear, the court can transmit this letter to the illiterate people of India tomorrow in a suitable way.

As the Chief Justice of India cannot do anything due to conflict of interests, this letter is submitted to *Justice A.K. Sikri*. As he is to retire very soon, he can do his duty and put right the public wrongs.

Due to the extraordinary conditions, the copy of this letter is submitted to the President of India and the Chief Minister of Tamil Nadu State. They can also publish this letter through the media.

# 53

# The discovery

A Delhi Court today (28 January 2019), granted bail to the former Chief Minister of Bihar, *Mr. Lalu Prasad Yadav*, in the IRCTC case.

The Prime Minister's Office (PMO) had asked former CBI Director *Mr. Alok Varma* to keep him jail till his death. None knows whether he is in jail or not now. Whatever happened, he might not have obtained bail from this case but for the revelation of *Mr. Alok Varma* and the timely letters of the present man.

*Mr. Jayakumar*, a minister in the Tamil Nadu State, diluted the stand of his Government against the striking employees at 11.30 A.M today (28-1-2019). The Madurai Bench of the Madras High Court, at 4 P.M. after consultation with the Chief Justice of India, asked the Government of Tamil Nadu to invite the employees for talks. It added that the Government is creating more and more problems by recruiting new hands. At 6 P.M. there were reports that the Education Minister would make a statement. The indications are that the strike would be withdrawn tomorrow. It must be noted that none lost any life or limb due to the strike.

If the conclusion of the present man is a correct one, the President of India, *Justice A.K. Sikri* and all other judges of the Supreme Court of India including the Chief Justice of India, Madurai Bench of the High Court, Chennai, and the ministers, Chief Minister of Tamil Nadu included, must be commended for their sincere and swift action to avert a Somalia like condition in the Tamil Nadu State.

The Prime Minister of India, *Mr. Narendra Modi*, today said that the efforts made by the Election Commission of India (ECI) is strengthening the Indian democracy.

The Prime Minister of India, *Mr. Narendra Modi* does not show his face to the people through the media. Congress Leader *Mr. Rahul Gandhi* also does not project himself before the people through the media. It is the Supreme Court of India that projects them to the people round the clock through the media. It will be 100 percent true after the declaration of the elections.

The people don't know any alternative to *Mr. Modi* other than *Mr. Rahul Gandhi*. They lost their ability to connect *Mr. Rahul Gandhi* with the Delhi and Mumbai Airports or with the money in the Provident Fund and the Pension Fund due to the Supreme Court of India.

Therefore, it is not the media that controls the public mind in India. It is the Supreme Court of India that controls the public mind in India. **It is the discovery of the present man after sending 698 letters to it.**

Otherwise, the court might have released the letters to the media and it might have taken appropriate measures for compliance.

In fact, the Supreme Court of India can either give democratic rights to the people or take away their rights.

The act of conducting the General Election before informing this work to the people is like dismembering the Constitution of India.

Therefore, the Supreme Court of India must restrain the ECI from conducting the elections before informing this work to the people. It is not for an interference in the governance of the country but for the freedom of the people to vote in the election.

The court need not think that the people would look down on **it for concealing 698 letters.**

**The basic tenant of a judge is that he will be able to look at the issue objectively.** Whether he looks at the issue objectively or not depends upon him. But the people must expect a reasonable decision from him based upon the true merits of the issue.

The people must expect the judge that **his decision or judgement will be based upon what is and what is not required by the Constitution of India and 'there is only limited room, if any at all, that he would be influenced by any ill-will'.**

The court might say that the present man would not win the confidence of the people even if freedom is given to them. It might say that *Mr. Mr. Narendra Modi* and *Mr. Rahul Gandhi* cannot be unseated in India.

But it is said that 'the most significant difference between civilization and savagery is **the willingness of the civilized men and nations to submit their differences to a factual test'.**

This is letter No.699.

This letter is being submitted to *Justice Aravid Bobde* for necessary action. Because of the extraordinary situation a copy is extended to the President of India and another copy to the Chief Minister of Tamil Nadu State.

# 54

# Misleading the people

Congress President *Mr. Rahul Gandhi*, on 28 January 2019, declared that he would implement '*a minimum income guarantee scheme*' if voted to power. He added that no one would remain hungry during his rule.

It is a clever idea. It shows that the leaders would vie with one another to do some good things to the people.

The newspapers all over India published his words as front-page headline news. The TV channels also gave equal importance. For the first time, the Supreme Court of India gives equal importance to him and Prime Minister *Mr. Narendra Modi.*

There was a time when the coolies did not get any work even for two days per week. The present man repeatedly pointed out this in these letters. To add weight to it, an incident that happened during the reign of

King Marthanda Varma of Travancore Kingdom was narrated. The King did not waste the physical labor of even one man in his kingdom.

The then Prime Minister of India, *Dr. Manmohan Singh,* implemented a scheme called Mahatma Gandhi Rural Employment Scheme. According to this scheme, anyone would get 100 man-days work per year. It is approximately two man-days work per week. It was based on the problem mentioned by the present man

Did Mahatma Gandhi tell this to Dr. Manmohan Singh?

Similarly, the present man gave a suggestion to give an identity number - like the Social Security Number in the USA- to every citizen of India. But the Government under *Dr. Manmohan Singh* called it Aaadhar.

The Service Tax was introduced based on the first letter dated 1-6-2001.

The transaction tax was suggested by the present man in the early letters. It was implemented by the then *Union Finance Minister, Mr. P. Chithambaram.* He gave another name to it. He chose a name from an economics book. He withdrew it after one year because *Mr. Yaswant Sinha* attacked it.

The present man did not suggest demonetization. When *Prime Minister Mr. Narendra Modi* did it, the present man requested him to disclose the brain behind the idea. He chose not to reveal it. Later, there were reports that the idea belonged to *Mr. Subramonia Swamy.*

Now, *Mr. Rahul Gandhi* must tell whether it is his idea or the one taken from this work. The reason is that it is the dominant theme of this work.

There are reports, that the Election Commission of India (ECI) is making transfers as a preparation for the election. The Chief Justice of India must reinstate former CBI Director, *Mr. Alok Varma.* He should not do what Prime Minister of India *Mr. Narendra Modi did.*

The Striking employees of the Government of Tamil Nadu returned to duty today (29-1-2019). What the present man knows is his last two letters and the present result. What happened in between is only an imagination.

If the last two letters catalyzed the changes, the present man must once again thank the President of India, *Justice Aravind Bobde,* the Chief Justice of India, the learned judges of the Supreme Court of India, Chief Minister of Tamil Nadu and his ministers provided they acted in good faith.

The strike cited by the present man in all three occasions ended within 24 hours of sending the letters. In another college teacher's strike, the politics of the present man clicked the issue although it has no concreate evidence.

In the *Miss. Anitha episode* and in the *Justice Karnan issue,* the President of India was not quick enough to act and thus the present man failed.

This shows that the present man could help solve some very serious problems. Should not the people all over India know this? Why did the Supreme Court of India fail to publish it as a headline news as in the case of *Mr. Rahul Gandhi* or *Prime Minister Mr. Narendra Modi?* Is it an ordinary thing for a man in the street? The court must ponder over it.

The striking employees demand pension just like their seniors, President of India, Members of Parliament (MPs), armed personnel and judges.

It is a problem that must be solved by the courts without delay. As the courts wriggle out from their responsibility, the employees stand in the streets.

Now, the crucial question before the Supreme Court of India is whether their demand is a constitutional one or not. If it is a constitutional one. the court must grant it. If not, it must deny it. There is no place in-between.

The present citizen of India would grant pension not only to the public servants but also to the private sector employees and all above 60 years using the money from the natural assets within 24 hours of assuming power as the Prime Minister of India. This is not a sudden inspiration. It is the dominant theme of this work from letter No.1 to letter No.700.

*Prime Minister Mr. Modi* might consider it as a daydream. If so, the Supreme Court of India may publish this letter giving as much importance as given today to the suggestion of *Mr. Rahul Gandhi.* Then all governments would accept it within a month.

The elections, unless otherwise restrained by the Supreme Court of India, might be conducted by treating the people like animals.

But it is unconstitutional.

A citizen of India might like to buy a mango. Shall the court offer him an apple or an orange?

Political rights must be given to the people before conducting the elections.

Now, the Supreme Court of India *projects Mr. Narendra Modi* and *Mr. Rahul Gandhi* as the prime ministerial candidates. Either a citizen must vote for *Mr. Modi* or for *Mr. Rahul Gandhi.* If it is democracy, the democracy in North Korea is a far better than this one.

Why do the judges of the Supreme Court of India project *Mr.Modi* and *Mr. Rahul Gandhi* and conceal the present man?

**If the judges of the Supreme Court of India make any untrue statement of a material fact to the 1300 million people, it is against their professional responsibility, if not an offence.**

**Similarly, if they omit to state a material fact to the people, then also it is against their professional responsibility, if not an offence.**

**These are the basic things in law education.**

**The judges now keep 700 letters from one citizen alone. It is a material fact. It is their responsibility to inform this to the people.**

**If they fail to do this before the election in appropriate doses, they would be mis-leading the people to make a wrong choice while determining their destiny.**

This is letter No.700. It is submitted to Justice Ramana of the Supreme Court of India for necessary action. A copy is submitted to the President of India and another copy is submitted to the Chief Minister of Tamil Nadu.

# 55

# Must obey whether one approves it or not

A bench of the Supreme Court of India headed by *Chief Justice of India Ranjan Gogoi* yesterday (30-1-2019) asked *Mr. Karthi Chithambaram,* son of former *Union Minister Mr. P. Chithambaram,* to deposit Re.10 crore - in the Aircel-Maxis case- to go abroad.

The Chief Justice of India handed over the Delhi and the Mumbai airports to private parties. He gave Re. 3 lakh crore rotting in the Provident Fund to unknown people. He gave away another Re.3 lakh crore to the same people. He secretly handed over the natural assets to the private parties. These were the tribute paid to unknown people to make **Mr. Rahul Gandhi** a national leader.

Then, he gave Re.59000 crore to some people in the pretext of gas subsidy and an equal amount of money in the pretext of an offset clause.

These were some of the tributes paid by the Chief Justice of India to keep **Mr. Narendra Modi** in the mind of the people.

The present Chief Justice of India might say that it is not correct on the part of the people to level such charges against him. But, he was not oblivious of such illegalities. The present man pointed out these to him, and to the earlier chief justices as and when they happened.

When a citizen of India seeks appropriate action for  deliberate violations to the Article 39 and the Article 19 of the Constitution of India from the Chief Justice of India, it becomes a direction that **the Chief Justice of India must obey whether he approves it or not.**

**The Chief Justice of India cannot change the Constitution according to his sense of equity. He must fall in line with the language of the Constitution of India.**

In fact, on 3 March 2003, the High Court, Kerala said, *"Whenever, there was violation of Constitution, the courts could not be silent spectators. They are under duty to intervene. The courts have no vested interests. They are not wedded to any valuables. They are sworn in to discharge their function without any fear or favor".*

Anyone would tell that in comparison to the offences committed by *Mr. Rahul Gandhi* and *Mr. Narendra Modi,* the above case of *Mr. Karthi Chitham* is an insignificant one. Is he being pursued for any other bigger offence? Nothing is clear.

One day, the Supreme Court of India observed *"We are not concerned whether the offender is a Minister, M.P. or M.L.A. this court is of the view that the investigating agencies should have no classification of offenders and book all persons - who are reasonably accused of committing crime. The court is further of the view that there should be only one category of offenders and not categories".*

Now, the Chief Justice of India projects *Mr. Narendra Modi and Mr. Rahul Gandhi*-through the media- as two prime ministerial candidates of India and proceeds against *Mr. Karthi Chithambaram,* son of former Union Minister *Mr. P. Chithambaram.*

*Prime Minister Mr. Narendra Modi* and *Congress President Mr. Rahul Gandhi* did violence against Article 39 of the Constitution of India. They do violence against Article 19 to float like only two leaders of India. They are accused persons. They do not deny it because they cannot deny it.

1300 million people of India want democracy. These two accused persons wants to become prime ministers after taking away the democratic rights of the 1300 million people.

There was a time when the media was controlling the judges of the Supreme Court of India. This work has slowly but steadily rescued them from its hand.

Now, the media is under the total control of the Chief Justice of India. In fact, he is holding it in his left hand. If he had directed it to report men and matters according to degree and ignore the offenders of Article 19, it might have obeyed promptly.

This letter is being submitted to *Justice Abhay Manohar Sapre* of the Supreme Court of India for necessary action. A copy is extended to the President of India and another copy to the Chief Minister of Tamil Nadu.

# 56

# Arresting the chief justices

The interim Union Budget was presented to the Parliament today (1-2-2019).

As predicted day-before-yesterday, there were many welfare schemes.

There was a suggestion to pay a pension of Re.3000 per month to every unorganized worker to benefit about 10 crore workers. But, it has a screw. It is that the worker must pay Re. 100 per month for certain years. What will he get tomorrow?

If the unorganized workers would get pension, is it possible for the Government of Tamil Nadu to deny pension to its employees?

The present man has been fighting for universal pension for all above 60 years for the last 18 years. The Government named it as the Prime Ministers Pension scheme. If there is a name for the *Universal*

*Pension Scheme,* the Government would call it Mahatma Gandhi Pension Scheme - as in the case of Mahatma Gandhi Rural Employment scheme!

Income Tax slab was raised from Re.2.5 lakh to Re.5 Lakh.  There must be another screw in it because the Minister did not present it in a straightforward manner.

The Government has a plan to sell Public Sector Undertakings (PSUs) for Re. 80,000 crore. The Minister did not tell the reason for it.

The Government can buy or sell anything without violating Article 39 and the Article 19 of the Constitution of India.

There are reports that the Government of India withheld the pension and retirement benefits of former Central Bureau of Investigation (CBI) Director, *Mr. Alok Varma,* for not reporting to duty after his transfer.

"You could not earn anything after working for more than 35 years. You could not buy even a bangle for me after marriage. You sold my property in the pretext of daughter's marriage. You did not spend the money for the marriage. You used it to clear your debts. I thought that you would buy a Dimond earring after retirement. I am not going to get even a gold ring. Did you ever give me anything after marriage? I am also a woman. I have my desires.

Do you want to beg in the streets? I will l not sit in the house, if you torment may son for money.

Do you know, how officers work? When they wanted to sell the Air India, that officer suggested to sell the remaining airports also. If they wanted to keep *Mr. Lalu Prasad Yadav* in jail, you should have arrested at least 10 more leaders in the opposition parties for disproportionate assets. None would come out of the jail, sir. You should have talked like this. What is the use in being an IPS officer? Will they give Nobel Prize for disobeying illegal orders? A man must have practical wisdom to survive in this world". His wife moaned like this to-day.

What the present man knows is his revelation and the impounding of his retirement benefits. Others are an imagination only.

Now, the officers will understand the language that they must use when they leak the inner secrets. They will sing a song before opening their mouth. They will lean on them for anything. They know the price they will have to pay if they refuse to obey illegal orders. They will understand the power of the Prime Minister of India.

The present man sent 702 letters to the Supreme Court of India for the freedom of Indians since June 2001. *Chief Justice of India Ranjan Gogoi* is omitting to state this material fact to the people of India.

The letters are necessary to the voters to take a balanced decision at the time of voting.

But, they do not know such omission on the part of the Chief Justice of India.

The Chief Justice of India knew that his such untruth or omission to state the material facts would mislead the people to vote in favor of two persons accused of violating Article 19 of the Constitution of India. He knew that such omission on his part would make him liable to all Indians.

**Therefore, the rule of law demands that the present Chief Justice of India, *Ranjan Gogoi*, and all Chief Justices of India since June 2001, must be arrested and prosecuted for their liability to all Indians.**

All prime ministers since June 2001 and all members of their Cabinet since June 2001 must be detained till the completion of the election process.

Former Congress President *Mrs. Sonia Gandhi,* Congress President *Rahul Gandhi* the secretaries of the Communist Party of India (M) since June 2001 also must be detained for their abetment to the crime.

These steps must be completed at least four months before the election.

These are the minimum requirements to conduct a free and fair election.

This is letter No.703

The Chief Justice of India cannot dispose of this letter due to conflict of interests. Therefore, it is submitted to *Justice A.K. Sikri* of the Supreme Court of India.

He need not indulge in any illegal concealment of this letter because it is an issue of all Indians. Any evidence of concealment would make the matters more complicated because of the Constitution of India. It is his constitutional prerogative to take any decision consistent with the Constitution of India.

As the people do not know anything, the contents of the letter may be informed to all Indians tomorrow.

A copy is submitted to the President of India and another copy is submitted to the Chief Minister of Tamil Nadu.

# Bibliography

1.Constitution of India drafted by Dr.B.R. Abedkar and the Drafting Committee of the Constituent Assembly of India signed by 284 members of the Constituent Assembly of India.

2. Class Actions by Herbert B. Newberg, Thomson West 2002.

3.How Arbitration Works by Martin M. Volz, by Edward Goggin (Editor), Martin M. Volz, Alan Miles Ruben (Editor)

4. Marthanda Varma by C.V. Raman Pillai, Translated from Malayalam by B.K. Menon, Sahitya Akademi: Reprint 1998, Rabindra Bhavan,35, Ferozesshah Road, New Delhi 110001

5.Political Thought By C.L. Wayper, English Universities Press, St. Paul's House, Warwick Lane, London, E.C. 4

6. Travancore Manual by V. Nagam Iiya, Travancore Government Press, Trivandrum

7.Prime Minister Mr. A.B. Vajpayee and the Abdication of power by Sabarimuthu.V. through  Amazon.com

8. The warring among Dr.A.P.J. Abdul Kalam, Dr.Manmohan Singh and Mrs. Sonia Gandhi by Sabarimuthu.V.  through Amazon.com

9. A. Madonna of India, Volume 1 by Sabarimuthu. V. through Amazon.com

10. A. Madonna of India, Volume 2 by Sabarimuthu. V. through Amazon.com

11. Thus Spoke Zarathustra, Nietsche, Translated with a Preface by WALTER KAUFMANN, Penguin Books

12. World Book of Encyclopaedia.

13. New Encyclopaedia by Funk & Wagnalls

14. The Pranab Effects by V. Sabarimuthu, Amazon.com

15, Newspapers –The New Indian Express, The Hindu, The Times of India, Deccan Chronicle and BusinessLine

16. Wikipedia

# Curriculum Vitae of the Author
## Sabarimuthu V

26-3 Thattankonam, Vellicode, Mulagumoodu PO, PIN : 629167

Email: sabarimuthu.vyakappan@gmail.com

## Academic Qualification

**M. Sc (Chemistry)** : Mar Ivanios College, Trivandrum, India (1973)

**B Sc (Chemistry)** : Scott Christian College, Nagercoil, India (1971)

## Profession

**Lecturer of Chemistry:** Lekshmipuram College of Arts and Science, Neyyoor, India (1974 - 2007)

## Publication

'Consolidated report on the National Adult Education Programme (1980)':

This publication was considered as a pioneering work in the field of adult education and was distributed to all universities and 700 and odd colleges all over India by the then adviser to the Government of India, Prof. L.R. Shaw, as a model.

## Self - book publication through the IJDJ Publications

'An Unconventional Approach to Inorganic Chemistry (1994)':

The American International Publishers (AIP) undertook a review of this book and described it as 'a valuable addition to the resources of educators'. It is a recognized reference book for the chemistry students of the M.S. University, Tirunelveli.

## Self-book publication through Amazon.com

**English**

1. English Grammar

2. A New English Grammar for the Beginners.

3. The Predicate Theory

**Chemistry**

1. Atomic Structure

2. Atoms, Ions, Environment and Reactivity

3. The Transition Elements

**History**

Ananthapadmanabhan

**Contemporary History**

1. Momentous Months

2. 13 Months in Office.

3. Prime Minister Mr. A.B. Vajpayee and the Abdication of Power (323 pages)

4. The Warring Among Dr. A.P.J. Abdul Kalam, Dr.Manmohan Singh and Mrs. Sonia Gandhi (812 pages)

5. A. Madonna of India, Volume 1 (595 pages)

6. A. Madonna of India Volume 2 (588 pages)

7. The Pranab Effects, Volume 1 (417 pages)

8. 'We will strange you' Volume 1 (382 pages).

9. Chief Justice Ranjan Gogoi

<u>**Social work**</u>

The students of the Tamil Medium RC Middle School in my village, Vellicode, lagged behind other schools in English, At the instance of the Headmaster, voluntarily taken English grammar classes to them for seven years at the rate of about 20 classes of 45 minutes duration per year. This school has been securing the first rank among about 100 schools in the last five years.

Further, these classes led to profound **The Predicate Theory** to the English Grammar. This theory, in contrast to the conventional **Verb Theory,** is a boon to all English learners all over the world. It can be discerned from the last 18 classes uploaded in the YouTube.

Conducted some English grammar classes at two other schools – Primary School, Pilankalai and High School, Pilankalai for five months each.

## Political work

645 letters have been sent to the President of India and the, Supreme Court of India since June 2001 for the freedom of Indians consistent with the Constitution of India.

## The most important blog

www.howeverythinghappenedinindia.blogspot.com

## YouTube videos

Videos on **English Grammar Classes, Chemistry Classes, some speeches on Politics and Economics** have been uploaded in the YouTube. The YouTube channel link is given below. There are 114 videos.

https://www.youtube.com/channel/UCBZWHucZhQsy6eqysw_7gvg?view_as=subscriber

# Acknowledgements (common to all books)

The publication of many books might not have happened without the valuable co-operation and assistance of all the members of my family consistent with their capabilities and opportunities. My wife, M. Stella Bai, is virtually a co-author, elder son S. James, younger son S. Delight, elder daughter S. Irene and her husband John Franklin, younger daughter S. Jasmine Madonna and her husband B. Godwin Bright and even my grand – daughter J. Jessica Lauren helped me in one way or other. Contributions of James and Delight are outstanding. All are entitled to very special acknowledgement and thanks.

Many in my family reared me for my education. Not a day passes without remembering my father, Mr. T.Vyakappan, mother, Mrs. R.Viyakulamarial, uncle Mr. R.Maria Michael, aunt Rev.Sr. R. Veronica, aunt Mrs.R. Theresammal and her husband Mr. Devasahayam, uncle Mr. T. Maria Soosai B.A. B.L. and his wife, and  Bishop of Vellore Rt. Rev. Antony Muthu,  uncle Mr. R.Maria Sebastian and his wife Mrs. Thangammal. Uncle Maria Mickael, in particular, stood like a rock for my education after my PUC.

Dr. John D.K. Sunder Singh and his brother, Jaya Singh, admitted me in the Scott Christian College, Nagercoil. Arch Bishop Most. Rev. Benedict Mar Gregories granted me admission in the Mar Ivanios College, Trivandrum for post-graduation.

Mr. Jesuadimai contractor, Mr. A. Pauliah M.L.A, State Bank of India Mr. Regunandana Kumar, Mr. A. Sankaranaraynan, Member of Syndicate, Madurai Kamaraj University, State Bank of India Mr. Paul Varnan, Mr. Devasahayam IAS helped me for my progress.

I remember with respect Mr. Maria Arulappan, Mr. Dhadachayini Amma, Mr. Innasimuthu, Mr. C. Francis, Mr. Soosai Muthu, Mr. Arulappan, Mr. A.Israel, S. Parameswari Amma, Mr. Maria Nesan Nadar M.A. B.T,, Mr. Moni, Mr.John I. James B.A. B.T, Mr. Revindra Nath B.Sc, B.T.,Mr. Sthanunathan Thambi, Mr. Retna Money B.Sc, B.T.Mr. V. Thomson, Mr. Theodore I.J. Kumarsingh M.Sc. Mr. R.S.A. Sunder Singh M.Sc. Mr.I.. Stalin M.Sc, Dr. V.S.David Raj M.Sc, Ph.D., Dr. Nambisan M.Sc.PhD. Dr. Scaria M. Chakalackal M.Sc, Ph.D. Mr, Ramasamy M.Sc. Prof. George M. Varghese and all my other great teachers.

Many in my wife's family are a source of encouragement and happiness. My father-in-law Mr. A. Martin, Mother-in-law-Maria Retnam, brother - in-laws- Mr. Robin Edward Martin B.Sc, Mr. Clement Joe Martin and Dr. Leenus Jesu Martin M.E. Ph.D. and father-in-law's brother Rev. Fr. A. Jockim and many others take great pride in my achievements. Further, I respectfully acknowledge the happiness of my close relatives, Mrs. Philomena, Mrs. and Mr. T. Retna Swamy M.A., Mrs. and Mr. Bright Xavier M.A. and Mrs. and Mr. Xavior Oscar Dhas M. Sc.

I think of the selfless services of Mr. P. Thankaswamy, Mr. Sundaram Pillai, founder Secretary and founder Director respectively of the Lekshmipuram College, Neyyoor.

I remember Thiruvatti Mr. C.Antony Joseph, Swamithara Vilai Mr.A.Arulappan, Madathattuvilai Mr. Soosai Michael, Erattan Vilai Mr. Innasimuthu, Kattuvilai Mr. Sabariyaradimai, Mr. S. Joseph, Kizhakkuvilai Mr. Michael, Vellicode Mr. R. Muthaiah B.Com, Mr. I. Sabarimuthu B.E., Erattan Vilai Mr. Mariakkon and all other members of the 'Gent's Federation' Vellicode for inculcating a reading habit in my early days.

I gratefully remember Dr.Achan Alex, Dr. Maman Thomas and Dr. Venugopalan Nair of Medical College, Trivandrum, Dr. Rajendra Retnam, Medical College, Tirunelveli, Dr. Dilip Pande, VHS Chennai, Dr. Sebasan, Dr. George, Dr. Selvam, Dr. Arun, Dr. S. Anto ENT, Dr.S.Rex M.D.S., Dr.S.K.Ranjith Kuman MS and all other selfless doctors.

I respectfully remember Kizhakkuvilai Mr. Varuvel Nadar and my relation, Pulippanam Mr. Devaraj.

I acknowledge my great colleagues - Mr. A. Francis, Mr. C. Bhagavandhas M.A., Mr. Edwin Sam M.A., Mr. A.M. Mathew M.Sc. C. Augustine M.A. Mr. Anantharaman Iyer M.Sc.Mr. Russel Raj M.A., Mr. Issac M.A., Librarian Mr. Kumaavel Renganathan, Librararian Mr. Saravanan Dr. Padmanabhan M.A. Ph.D, Dr. Ramalingam Pillai M.Sc. Ph.D, Dr. Sukumaran M.Sc, Ph.D., Mr. Ravikumar M.A., Dr. David Raja Bose M.A. Ph.D., Mr. Neelakandan M.A. Dr. Jayakumar M.A. Ph.D., Dr. Sreekandan M.A. Ph.D in the Lekshmipuram College, Neyyoor and my friends –E.M. Edward Joseph M.Sc, Mr. Thavethu, Mr. Kuttinadan, Kizhakkuvilai Yesudhason,

Kizhakkuvilai Mr. V. Laurence, Mr. Melavilai Thobias, Puthuvilai Mr. Rajendran, Kattuvilai Mr.Sabariyaradimai, Mr.M. Gopalan M.A, B.L.Advocate, Mr. Nesaiyan teacher, Mr. Thanka Raj M.A. B.Ed  and Mr. Devasahayam teacher.

Lekshmipuram College Principal Mrs. Daisy David M.A. appointed me as the Programme Officer of Adult Education. It was a turning point in my career. My publication on the National Adult Education Programme (NAEP), 1980, was distributed to 80 universities and 700 and odd colleges all over India by Prof. L.R.Shah, the then adviser to the Government of India, This boosted my self-confidence and the standing among the teachers. I must thank them. In fact, it was a great motivation to do more and more.

Headmaster Mr. Irudhayadhason gave me a chance to teach English Grammar to children. I utilized it to demolish the core area of English grammar and constructed a new one. It is not possible to explain the essence of English grammar in a reasonable way without my book. No one has disputed this claim. It gives me great satisfaction. I am indebted to him.

The Indian political system comprising the successive Presidents since Mr. K. R. Narayanan and virtually all political leaders contributed their share for my development in one way or other. Many leaders like Mr. H.D. Deve Gowda, Mr. A.K. Antony acknowledged my letters for freedom. At one time, I dropped different letters to more than 250 Members of Parliament. I could not contact all due to practical difficulties. Barring one political leader, all leaders digested my letters without the slightest disagreement.

Prime Minister of England Mr. Tony Blair, Prime Minister of England Gordon Brown, Prime Minister of the Netherlands Dr.Dr. Jan Peter Balkenende, Her Royal Highness the Queen of Travancore Gouri Lekshimi Bai and many other world leaders acknowledged and gave their opinions to my letters for freedom. Her Royal Highness Queen Elizabeth 'lighted fire' on two occasions. I described her as a Madonna of England. The Emperor of Japan 'lighted fire' as mentioned in the book, 'A Madonna of India'.

I sent many letters by post to the learned judges of the Supreme Court of India since June 2001. I thought that they would revolt against the BALCO judgment. It did not happen. Then I sent 561 emails to the Supreme Court of India, President of India, Central Bureau of Investigation (CBI), Central Vigilance Commission (CVC) and Election Commission of India (ECI). Several emails were sent to the Indian Army, Indian Air Force and many others. Then I stopped sending the emails to them. After that a few letters were sent to the Secretary General of the United Nations (UN). After Mr. Ram Nath Kovind assumed power as the President of India, I remained quiet for a few months. But he alienated the Essar Oil to Russia. He could not do anything in the matter of entrance examination or to give any relief to Justice Karnan. Further, Finance Minister Mr. Arul Jaitely said that privatization is an art in India and started taking speedy steps to alienate the Air India. Therefore, I resumed sending emails to  the President of India with great intensity pointing out his constitutional duty and concentrated my attention to convert my works into books through Amazon.com.

On 12 January 2018, four out of five senior most judges of the Supreme Court of India came out and 'lighted fire' saying that democracy was in peril. What I expected in 2002 happened in 2018! It was the first press conference of judges ever in the history of India.

This means that 80 per cent of the judges agree that there is no democracy or constitutionalism in India.

India is replete with intellectuals. There are many great achievers in India. However, this work is a great achievement for the 1000 million people of India. That I could achieve it without a word of support from the media is a source of great satisfaction.

I repeatedly sought the help of the media all over the world in the fond hope that due publicity would bring freedom to Indians.

When a girl in Tamil Nadu committed suicide protesting the NEET, I sent an email each to virtually all newspapers and TV Channels all over the world again in vain. The media simply steered the attention of the people to other matters.

Notwithstanding everything, the soil of my village, Vellicode, the college I worked - Lekshmipuram College, Neyyoor - and India is responsible for my growth.

Sabarimuthu.V.

India

9-2-2019